Dr. Rye Bell

DANCE

WITH THE

TRINITY

Pursuing God in Spirit & Truth

Post Gutenberg™

AN IMPRINT OF
GLOBALEDADVANCEPRESS

Dance with the Trinity: *Pursuing God in Spirit and Truth*

Copyright © 2011 by Jesse Rye Bell
Library of Congress Control Number: 2011936564
Bell, Jesse Rye 1953 –

> Dance with the Trinity: Pursuing God in Spirit and Truth
> ISBN978-1-935434-06-1

> Subject Codes and Description:
> 1: REL012000: Religion: Christian Life - General 2: REL012040:
> Religion: Christian Life - Inspirational 3: REL012120: Religion:
> Christian Life – Spiritual Growth.

Cover design concept by Brian Lane Green

Produced in the United States of America

Published by
Post-Gutenberg Books™
An Imprint of GlobalEdAdvancePRESS

www.gea-books.com

This book is dedicated to my dear wife, Becky.
Through her loving support, my personal
Dance with the Trinity
has deepened and become graceful.

I love you beyond measure and words.

Acknowledgments

A head-scratcher simply means something I don't understand. How can a person find enjoyment in reading and re-reading a manuscript for the purpose of pursuing excellence? Sharon Latran challenged my thoughts to be sure that what I longed to convey actually appeared on the printed page, graciously exhibiting patience as she walked with me through this effort. No words are adequate enough to express my thankfulness for all she has done.

There are so many other individuals in my life that deserve a spot on this page of recognition. My family, especially my father and Aunt Berdie, as well as many of my friends who understand the teachings on "One Another" in God's Word. Relationships like these are rare. I am so thankful that my family and friends are courageous and bold in their spirit. I am blessed that they have been willing to share their lives with me in this way. To each one of you I simply wish to say: "I love you." "Thank you so very much."

Table of Contents

Preface

How To Use This Book

The objective of this book, as well as being a good read, is to serve as a study guide directing the reader through a process of understanding relationships as they can and should be with God and with man. The hope is that this book will serve as a firm foundation or "solid ground" on which to build even deeper studies and a pursuit of God.

The effort is to teach about relationships through examples in the reading portion of this book. Then, through studying what the Bible has to say about this topic, move the reader to a deeper, more personal knowledge of relationship. It is my hope that the reader will develop a deeper understanding about how to let God's Word transform them into Christ's image.

The study part of this book is set up in such a way that both the new Christian and the mature in Christ Jesus will be able to search the Scriptures and make direct application to their lives. The references of specific passages in Scripture do not give exact answers but allow for each individual to make personal application of what the main focus is and what that passage is trying to teach or convey.

As you complete the reading portion of each chapter it is suggested that you follow up with the accompanying Bible study before moving on to the next chapter. In approaching the book in this way one can more successfully make the connection between the given examples and the teaching of God's word.

Unless it is indicated otherwise, the Bible quotations in this book are from the New American Standard Bible version (NASB). Use any translation you would like for study, preferably more than one for comparison. However, a paraphrase, such as the Living Bible or the Good News Bible, is not accurate enough for study when used alone.

You are encouraged to READ the Scriptures thoroughly and spend some time thinking about their contents before trying to answer the questions in the study portion. Go back and re-read the passages in an attempt to INTERPRET as you provide answers to the questions. Lastly, spend time meditating and memorizing what you have learned so that you will be able to APPLY this to daily life.

- READ

- INTERPRET

- APPLY

Foreword

Like a pocket of air that rises to the surface of a body of water, the experience of life forces questions of fundamental importance into our consciousness. Why am I here? Through whom or what or how did things come into existence? Is there a supreme being who is the author of all that exists? If there is a supreme being, what is his nature? Has he and does he communicate with us? Are we accountable to him? Can we come to know him, and does he know us?

Starting with the faith position that there is a God who created all that exists, Dr. Rye Bell helps us navigate through the testy questions that logically follow. His emphasis centers on the last question listed above – Can we come to know Him, and does He know us? If there is an area that should be emphasized within Christendom today, it deals with the answers to these two questions: "How do I come to know God intimately, and why should I seek this intimacy?"

Having served as a campus minister on a major university campus for almost 38 years, I have fielded on many occasions, questions that take a variation of this one – If I commit to Christ and give Him lordship over my life, what do I get out of it? The right answer is first of all "salvation," i.e., the forgiveness of sins, the entrance and the abiding of the Holy Spirit into one's life, and eternal life. As incredible as this good news is for us, God does offer even more to us! Students and others might like the more to be: a good job, a great looking soul mate, health, wealth, and influence. Such things may come, but it does a great injustice to imply that these add-ons will automatically follow a commitment to Christ. They may not follow at all.

What we can state for certain is that God does offer us intimacy. This is astounding! That the God of the universe invites us into a relationship of deep loving intimacy is almost beyond comprehension. This is what we should be telling prospective and active believers – God wants an intimate relationship with us! This is a gift of incalculable worth that far outstrips any other possible add-ons.

Dr. Bell, in his unique way, has focused on this remarkable offer of intimacy. He calls it "Dance with the Trinity." Refusing to sidestep difficult issues, he guides us through scriptural direction and insightful narrative to go further to find our place of intimacy with God. Rye is an alumnus of our campus ministry at the University of Tennessee. He has always been a seeker of God and has well qualified himself through his education and counseling practice to help us experience the joy of dancing with God. His is a needed message in a world of fractured relationships where intimacy is rarely achieved. In such a world, the offer of intimacy with God is indeed, great news!

Sam Darden, Director/Campus Minister
Campus Christian Ministry, Inc.
University of Tennessee – Knoxville, TN

Introduction
The Pursuit

Considering a book or a study guide like this one for a number of years, the initial motivating factor for such an undertaking sprang out of a personal word study searching the Scriptures for certain words that were vital in supporting the work I was doing in a Biblical Guidance ministry. Early in my counseling experience it was apparent to me that the authority of the Bible was absolutely essential in helping individuals come to a deeper understanding of their personal attempts at the *art of living well.*

Someone once said, "God's calling for you becomes evident when your deepest passion runs directly into one of the world's deepest needs." The world, both the saved and the lost, needs to have intimate relationship with God. Years spent listening to people discuss their lives in counseling settings have taught me to recognize faulty thinking that results in the development of faulty patterns. Usually these faulty patterns developed out of a deep desire to avoid future pain that could resemble a painful past. In this respect it is God's call for me to write about developing an intimate relationship with a Holy God. It is this call that directs me to write about learning to "Dance with the Trinity."

My early advanced studies took place in the secular realm of American society. I was a strong believer and held firmly to my Christian roots throughout educational pursuits. It was impossible to accept the flawed efforts within the "helping" profession that were based on false doctrine. In graduate school, questions to the pop quizzes were answered in ways that the professors were looking for, and then I would add some Biblical truth to the concept of the therapeutic intervention(s). As President of the Graduate School of Social Work, my GPA was near the top in my class. Even though deeply involved in the educational process, I realized that what the school was teaching fell far short of what was necessary to bring about true and lasting change in a person's life. I knew that the solid foundation of God's Word was the missing piece. It is the Truth found in His Word that is absolutely essential to the process of helping others.

Many hours have been spent studying, searching, and trying to understand what the Scriptures actually meant by Man (mankind) was created in the image of God. My study of God's Word and reading the works of theologians like C.S. Lewis, J.I. Packer, Andrew Murray, Charles Spurgeon, A.W. Tozer, John Piper, Watchman Nee, R.A. Torrey, Billy Graham, Martin Luther, G.K. Chesterton, Francis Schaeffer, and many others helped me come to an understanding of who Man is. In leading me toward that answer they also pointed to character qualities of God that help to form deeper thoughts about my Creator.

It has been through this intimate pursuit of God that I have come to the idea of sharing some of my studies. Hopefully, as one moves through the particular suggested Scripture passages at the end of each chapter their faith will begin to collide with the Majesty of God and His sovereignty. Facing the Majesty of

God and His sovereignty opens the path to developing a deeper understanding concerning intimacy in relationship with our Creator. It is my prayer that this will serve to motivate and at the same time equip individuals to an even deeper study that would last a lifetime.

Some of the words used in the book like *intimate, relationship, passion, dance, grace, and mercy* might jump off the page towards some of you more "manly men" as fluff. Let me stop right here and say that our culture, and more specifically the Christian church, has spent entirely too much of their time emasculating men. They have contributed in wrong, even sinful ways to the process of men no longer understanding what it means to be a man living boldly and courageously for God. While some of the words that are used are absolutely necessary to convey the point of this book, let me assure you that there can be no more courageous and manly a pursuit than the effort to become more Christ-like. It is manly to love God. The sacrificial love that is required in a relationship with our Creator is just too much for lesser men. It *is* manly to set an appropriate pace both emotionally and spiritually in your family. To do this according to God's design proves to be just too much for a weak man to handle. The truth is that we men need to understand more fully what it means to be in a "right" relationship with both God and mankind. We have been given positions of authority on purpose, certainly not by some oversight or accident by the Sovereign. So as you read this book you must be prepared to *man-up* to the most significant call of all: being the man that God has both called and designed you to be.

As you read through these pages, I hope that it becomes apparent how desperately God desires us and longs to invite us to "The Dance." This book/study looks at both the nature of Man and the nature of a Triune God (Father, Son, and Holy Spirit). Is there theology in this book? Absolutely! However, it is not a theological work. There is nothing about the purpose of this book that is meant to defend or argue points of Calvinism versus points of Arminianism or to take strong stands in support or against any denominational points of view. Many of man's theological debates become so focused on "being right" that it is common to find that the plain statements of the Bible have been ignored. To bring Christ-followers together in the love and unity of the Holy Spirit, this book/study is solely focused on the Word of God with a central theme of being in relationship one to another and in relationship with a Holy God.

It is my true desire that this tool can be used to stir, to equip, to motivate, and to encourage others to begin their own personal Dance with the Trinity.

Dr. Rye Bell

§

Part I
Why We Need Relationship

Better Together
Divine Jealousy

One

Better Together

Rick was thirty-eight years old. He was lying in the I.C.U. when I first met him. His condition had worsened over the past several days. His body was riddled with melanoma cancer, and new cancer nodes were popping up daily. Rick, like many other patients, could point to places on his body and tell his physician where the newly affected area was on each day. This is a relatively common phenomenon with medical patients. All hope for a physical recovery was now lost in Rick's life. He had not responded well to the radiation and chemotherapy, and now the cancer was requiring more and more from his body. This horrible disease was literally taking the life away from him. He was physically losing the battle.

Visiting Rick most every day, my role in his treatment was to have him educate me about his dying process. While that last statement might seem a bit odd, let me assure you that this approach proved to be a very valuable part of treatment.

For the past year I had been working closely with an anesthesiologist and an oncologist in their private practices. They had asked me as a Pastor and counseling professional focusing on Biblical Guidance to bring both a spiritual and intellectual piece into the overall treatment milieu of patients who had been diagnosed with terminal cancer.

There was something I realized early on in working with these individuals. Contrary to the popular belief that people generally do not want to talk about dying or an afterlife, the exact opposite was the case. While it was, at times, uncomfortable – discussing dying as a part of the life cycle was encouraging for most people. The more the topic was opened up the more a calmness and security developed in most of my patients.

There is no place that I know of that has as much integrity than on the hospital bed of a terminally diagnosed patient. All of the things that tend to distract and stifle us emotionally, relationally, volitionally, and rationally seem to disappear in the moment of intense focus on what it means to be human and the sober realization of our finiteness. Rick proved to be no different.

Rick had two beautiful children ages 3 and 5. Both of his girls were very much in love with their Daddy. Their ages prevented them from having a very deep understanding of what was ahead for them. Oh, they knew that their Daddy was sick, but they didn't understand the limitations that surrounded their situation and how very soon it would be when their Daddy was no longer going to be with them. There were times when the girls and their Mother would be in the room when I visited. These little girls would be sitting on the bed coloring and showing their Daddy their latest creations. Rick, in pain and usually completely exhausted, always had an encouraging smile for his children.

One day after they left Rick asked me a very unusual question. He said, "Rye, do you know when you are dead?" I wasn't sure how to respond. Was this dying man getting ready to tell me a joke that he had heard on *The Tonight Show* the evening before? Was he going to give me some "spiritual" insight to what he had learned during this painful journey? Was he going to tell me what God had spoken to him in a dream? I could only say, "No, Rick, I don't know when you are dead. When does that happen?" Rick responded, "When the nurses and other staff here at the hospital quit looking at you. When they come in your room and do their job and try to act like everything is normal, but everyone knows it isn't. It is like they know you have only a few days left, and they don't know how to have a relationship or say good-bye so they just don't talk or even look at you. You know, Rye, you would think that the medical community would be able to deal with death better than that wouldn't you?" Rick went on to say, "One of the things that I look forward to each day is your visit and the way that we share. It is during those times that I can talk about what others are afraid to discuss. We are able to talk about the things in life that truly matter. You have allowed me to live fully, knowing that I am dying. You have helped me to understand that I want to die with dignity. In doing so, I want to teach my daughters that facing death with surety is something that is not abnormal but is and should be the norm. I want them to know that my strength, even in death, comes from a God that loves me dearly. Rye, if they don't see that or are just too young to understand or remember, could you make sure they know this?" Rick died a couple of hours after that meeting.

There it is, the truth about life and relationship. This is the truth coming straight from the heart of a dying man that has already decided there is no need for pretense, no need for hidden meanings or verbal superficialities. In the words of Brennan Manning, "The *Imposter* is exposed and gone." All the games are over and nothing is left but absolute intimacy in relationship. It is this strong desire to know and to be known that goes beyond anything else. When all else becomes just substitutes for what it truly means to be both human and a child of the King of Kings, then what we are left with is a deep desire to have true intimacy in relationship both with our fellow man and with our God.

We Need Each Other!

Have you ever been out playing golf, just enjoying the day, drinking in all of the sunshine and cool breeze? Days like that are special. The only thing that could possibly make a day like that better is to sink a hole-in-one on that difficult par three that rarely gives even a par. If that elusive hole-in-one is hit, you better have someone there to verify your greatness, but, better yet, just to share in the joy of the moment. The joy of the moment always seems richer when you can share the accomplishment and the thrill of such an exciting time.

It was kind of like that for me the other day sitting in a Cracker Barrel restaurant playing the *peg* game:

> If you leave just one you are a *genius*, leave
> two and you're *purdy smart*, leave three and
> you're *jest plain dumb*, and leave four or more
> and you are *jest an ignoramoos*!

Well, wouldn't you know…I got them all out and left just one with no one to share my joy. I called the waitress over and did it again. She was *really impressed*! But, it just wasn't the same as if someone had been there to smile and say, "WOW!," "Way to go!," or "'Atta boy!"

Isn't that the way it is? We need each other. If for no other reason, we need each other to share in life. We don't often admit that or act like we have this deep desire but it's there all the same.

Jack Johnson has a song that is really popular these days called, "Better Together." Regardless of genre, this song and others that focus on human and Godly relationships find popularity in our culture. Songs about relationship zoom to the top of the charts. But, why do we love these tunes? What is their attraction? Well, the attraction exists because we possess within our souls, by God's Holy and perfect design, a deep, deep desire to know and to be known. This is true for our personal, human relationships but is especially true for our relationship with God.

Within our human relationships lie the struggle of knowing and of being known and the danger of taking that risk. Let me explain: Picture, if you will, your body just as it is with one small exception. All the way down the front of you, from head to toe, is a very large and secure zipper. If you were to "unzip" one could look into you and see all – behaviors and thoughts of past, present, and future. They could see and know the good and wonderful things about you. They would also be able to see and know those things about you that were not so good. And, they could even see and know those things that create for you the most shame and discouragement. They could see and know the wretchedness of your heart at its worst.

In our humanness our deepest desire, our deepest longing, would be to have the ability to be in relationship with others in such a way that being so exposed would be safe. Those who are special to us would be able to look inside of us and see all. After seeing all that can be seen, their loving response to everything – the good, the bad, and the horrific would be a simple and genuine – "I love you so very much!" You see, it is our deepest desire to be fully known and at the same time be in such a relationship as to be fully loved in the midst of our greatest and even most risky of all human endeavors, absolute honest exposure in a deep and meaningful, intimate relationship.

The problem occurs when our deepest desire, our deepest longing to be able to "un-zip," meets up with the fear of what could and probably will happen if we take this bold step in relationship. Our experience in human relationships is one of disappointment and mistrust. Those individuals that we should be able to trust and give our all, have let us down and proven that taking the step of pursuing relationship with passion is just not worth the high risk this step demands. In the midst of driving towards our deepest longing we are met face-to-face with our deepest fear.

It is in these tragic life experiences that we learn to stay on guard and hold our cards close to the chest. It is in these experiences that Satan the enemy of God will come. Satan's purpose for approaching is to convince us that not only can we not trust each other but that all relationships are untrustworthy. This risk and lack of trustworthiness, according to Satan, is not only real and dangerous in our earthly relationships, but this risk would also extend to our attempts at having intimate relationship with God. He does this by adding that one necessary ingredient to make a "con" or a scheme successful - truth. I know it sounds odd. But, in order for a con to work there needs to be enough truth in the lie to make it become *totally* believable. Satan, the prince of lies, the master of cons, uses our failed, earthly experience to speak about something that is both Heavenly and Spiritual and unrelated to our earthy failures. Satan's scheme is to make us realize our failures regarding relationships in general. Once Satan has successfully captured our attention with the truth of failures in relationship, he then extends his story of human trials and failures to include our relationship with God. It is in the "shift" that his lie is revealed and becomes an effort to deceive and destroy. Continuing to speak about relationship as it should be, man towards man, I will develop Man's relationship with God in subsequent chapters.

Our Heavenly Father counters the deceptive practices of Satan by revealing his intent for our lives by way of His written word. Because God desires not only to have relationship with us, and that we enjoy relationship with each other, the Christian Scriptures have some clear directives on how we are to live in community with one another. "One another" is an idea that runs throughout the New Testament. We have clear instruction and obligation to each other within the Body of Christ.

For example, Paul told Timothy to exhort and enlighten (teach, instruct) the believers in his local church (1 Tim. 4:12). Many other passages combine to suggest that encouragement, exhortation, and enlightenment are a primary responsibility of the local church. The local church is, by definition, a community of people who share a unique life and express their shared life in love for one another. Members of this group are to share their Spirit-granted abilities with the others. Every believer is able to encourage his brothers and sisters.

Living in *community* and sharing our lives with one another is a primary theme in the New Testament. Take a brief look at some of the scriptures that speak to this principle of Christian relationship with "one another."

"ONE ANOTHERING"

- John 15:12- Love one another
- Romans 5:13- Don't pass judgment on one another
- Romans 12:5- Be members of one another
- Romans 12:10- Honor one another
- Romans 12:10- Be devoted to one another
- Romans 12:16- Live in harmony with one another
- Romans 14:19- Build up one another
- Romans 15:5- Be like-minded toward one another
- Romans 15:7- Accept one another
- 1 Corinthians 6:6- Don't pursue lawsuits against one another
- 1 Corinthians 12:25- Care for one another
- Galatians 5:13- Serve one another in love
- Galatians 5:15- Don't spitefully hurt one another
- Galatians 5:26- Don't provoke or envy one another
- Galatians 6:2- Bear one another's burdens
- Ephesians 4:32- Be kind to one another
- Ephesians 5:21- Submit to one another
- Colossians 3:9- Don't lie to one another
- Colossians 3:13- Teach and counsel one another
- 1 Thessalonians 3:12- Abound in love toward one another
- 1 Thessalonians 4:18- Comfort one another
- Titus 3:3- Don't hate one another

- Hebrews 3:13- Encourage one another

- Hebrews 10:24- Stir up one another to love and good deeds

- James 4:11- Don't slander one another

- James 5:9- Don't bear grudges against one another

- James 5:16- Confess your sins to one another

- James 5:16- Pray for one another

- 1 Peter 4:9- Offer hospitality to one another

- 1 Peter 5:14- Greet one another

- 1 John 1:7- Have fellowship with one another

Go back and take another look at the "One Anothering" list. It strikes me that God's point is absolutely clear. Under His direction we are as a church to provide community for one another. It makes absolute sense that our God and Creator would know the basic need we have for relationship one to another in community. This need is part of who we are and is also a result of *Whose* we are having been created in God's image!

God truly desires us to have relationship with Him. Since we have been created in the image of God we also long for relationship with one another. It is true that by His perfect and holy design we are indeed "Better Together." The Scriptures spend much energy teaching us how to show love for each other. Our guide and pattern is the love that God has for us. We are instructed to use that very example of His love for us as a barometer for how we should be showing our love in relationship with others. Part of our passionate pursuit of God then would necessarily include our passionate pursuit of others in loving care, support, and discipleship.

The "zipper" example shows how we as individuals truly long to be in deep and meaningful relationship with each other. It reveals that while the longing is there, this longing is accompanied by a deeper fear of failure and rejection. This fact is proof of the spiritual warfare that you and I are involved in each day of our lives. It is that fear of pain in the midst of relationship that forces our hand to face this ultimate risk. It is that fear that serves as a valuable tool in Satan's arsenal of lies and deception in the midst of his ferocious attacks. Satan hopes that you and I are willing to live in that fear. If we choose to abide in that fear we can expect to experience only periodic success with harmony in our relationships. Even then in the pursuit of harmony we will lose all ability to discover intimacy with one another.

True intimacy in relationship requires risk. That risk comes in the form of humility and obedient submission to His lordship as we shape our lives into living sacrifices that are both holy and pleasing to our God. While the fear is real, you and I have to realize that the fear we have concerning relationship is not of God. We do experience deep emotion about relationship because in some sense all is on the line. The risk is huge because we can only be in intimate relationship through obedience to God. However, whether we are in obedience or not, our souls will always desperately long to have a safe place to land. From our very depths we hope to find protection and importance in intimate relationship with others. This is a universally true statement. It is equal among the sexes. It is a true statement within any culture, any age, any race, and religion. Every person longs to have relationship with others. It is true because this is how our Creator has designed us. The desire is a direct response to His plan.

Mankind is driven to be involved with each other, to try to have relationship one to another. God calls us to certain directives in our relationships in order to experience them to the fullest. It can and will be through our obedience to His Lordship that we know and experience this relationship as He has intended.

For Deeper Insight:

- If Jesus were to pray on your behalf, what 'one' thing would you most like Jesus to ask the Father to do for you?

- The Bible has a great deal to say when it comes to relationship. This applies not only to our relationship with God but also to one another within the body of believers. What responsibility do we have when it comes to being in relationship with each other as believers?

- In the passages found in 1 John 1:3, 7 what was John's purpose in sharing this wonderful news?

- In these three scripture references: Ephesians 5:2, 19, 30; Colossians 2:2; and Colossians 3:16, what is the overriding theme of encouragement or direction?

- What is the result of speaking about the Lord and encouraging others to live for God? See Malachi 3:16

- What is the result of being in the presence of God? See Psalm 55:14

- Look up the following passages of scripture: Acts 2:1, 42, 46-47; Romans 15:5-7; 1 Corinthians 1:10; Galatians 6:2, 10; Ephesians 2: 19-22; Philippians 1:3, 27, Philippians 2:1 6; Hebrews 10: 24-25. What is it that holds us together, and how should that influence how we treat those within our spiritual family?

- Take some time going back through the passages shared in the middle of this chapter about the "One Another's." Ask God to teach you to have an attitude that looks like Jesus. If you did take on a servant's spirit towards others, would it cause you to view yourself differently? How?

Two

Divine Jealousy

The desire to be in relationship is elementary. As already mentioned, this base level of our existence, to have and to be relational, is a primary part of what it means to be created in the image of God. The desire to belong, the desire to *fit in*, and the desire to create significant relationships is at the center, at the core, and at the heart of who we are.

While the last chapter spoke of how we desire to be in relationship with one another, I want to turn now to look at how much God desires to be in relationship with us.

God is indeed passionate for us. The problem is that many of us never take the time to consider just how passionate He is towards us. Because of this we tend to miss Him in relationship. We don't miss God entirely, but we do miss Him in the relationship as He intends.

It is certainly the minority who understand that God is the greatest of all lovers. Throughout the history of man, God has presented Himself as that of a wooing lover. We humans, we Christians, and especially the male gender of those two groups find it difficult to relate to or actually embrace the idea of God being our lover. Yet this idea of God pursuing mankind in romantic love is something that is frequently played out in all of Scripture. How else can scriptures such as those in Isaiah and Jeremiah be understood except through the eyes of a pursuing

lover?   "…as a young man weds a maiden, so you shall wed
him who rebuilds you, and your God shall rejoice over you
as a bridegroom rejoices over the bride," (Isaiah 62:5); and, "I
remember the devotion of your youth, how as a bride you loved
me…" (Jeremiah 2:2). How else can the books of Nehemiah and
Hosea be read and understood? I haven't even begun looking at
The Song of Solomon which is clearly the most romantic book
found in the Scriptures. There might be some who would argue
that the Song of Solomon is a love letter from a man to a woman.
I agree with that idea in part. However, since all of Scripture is
Christo-centric [centered around the person of Jesus Christ] it
is impossible to imagine that in the midst of all the Bible, God
would somehow decide to place some unrelated love letter to
merely stimulate us via a story of some heterosexual relationship.
I think not! While the Song that Solomon sings is of love to his
beloved, it is also the song our God is singing, and it reveals the
deep and intimate relationship that He longs to share with us,
His beloved children. It is true that God longs for intimacy in
relationship with us. He refuses to settle for mere harmony.

If you are one of the fortunate ones who have been allowed
to experience a true and passionate love here on this earth, you
will agree that much has been added to your life for having been
involved in such an experience. Prior to finding this *true love* you
lived and enjoyed life, as far as you knew, to its fullest. However,
once exposed to the reality of the deepest and truest of earthly
romantic loves you are able to clearly understand how much of
life you had actually missed. The partner of this romantic love
has brought a new dimension to you. That dimension was the
necessary ingredient that existed outside your personal being
but was still essential for you to be complete.

It is like that with God. Until we *fall in love* with God by coming to the point of understanding our spiritual poverty we will not be able to grasp the Kingdom of Heaven. It is God and God alone that can bring a dimension to our life that is necessary in order for us to be filled. We can study about God. We can say we love God. We can sing songs to God, and we can pray to God. However, until we submit humbly to His love by understanding that we are completely dependent on Him we will never know God fully. Just like earthy love requires humility, so does the ultimate of relationships found with our Creator.

The first of the Beatitudes says: "Blessed are the poor in spirit, for theirs is the kingdom of heaven" (Matthew 5:3). This Beatitude speaks to an attitude of falling in love with God through an understanding of our destitute spiritual nature. If a person has realized their own complete helplessness and has put their whole trust in God, their lives will experience change in two different ways. First, they will become turned-off by the imitations and cheap substitutes that come from material things and superficial relationships. The true spiritually poor person will know that the ability to find contentment and security in things of earth and the ability to comfortably settle in shallow relationship is just not there. The second event that will take place (by the way, simultaneously with the first) is a complete attachment to God. The person who understands his spiritual poverty will know that God alone can bring him the help that is needed for life. It is God alone that will bring the necessary strength and hope. This person will realize that God means absolutely everything and that things mean nothing at all. It is when we realize this that we begin to enter into intimacy with God.

Sadly within the church we sometimes settle. We *do* our Christianity by attending the Sunday service and complain when the drums are too loud or the sermon went beyond our appointed time. We leave the service expressing dismay that "we really didn't get anything out of the message." We show up at church expecting to receive. It doesn't dawn on us that we have come to give our all with others in corporate worship to the only One who is worthy. We meet in homes and discuss various letters written to First century churches and either marvel at their commitment to the cause of Christ or wonder how they could be so off base. We meet and never realize the applications that are available to us if we would only connect the obvious dots, the spiritual lesson for our own lives. The modern church with all its seeker sensitivity and entertaining programs has settled. In many cases the Church has settled for what amounts to a cheap imitation of familiarity instead of a passionate relationship with God. We speak of our love for God. We speak of our love for people. We become satisfied with what we have spoken.

If the course that we choose is to only speak of our love for God, God has clearly indicated that His response will be, "And then will I declare to them, I never knew you; depart from me, you workers of lawlessness" (Matthew 7:23). God will always refuse to accept our attempts to offer cheap substitutes to Him. God has given to us His very best. God knows for what purpose He has created us, and He accepts no less than His intent for relationship with us.

God Talk

It is important at this point to make a clear distinction about the term "God Talk" used in this and following chapters. When I speak of the term "God Talk" I generally mean those words that by their usage bring one to thoughts of God. There are words used in Christian culture not generally used outside that environment. Some examples would be: repentance, sanctified, propitiation, born-again, etc. In conversation we sometimes express the truthfulness of God's word with a faithful and obedient heart. All of these examples would be included in my definition of good or appropriate God Talk. However, there is a negative side to this God Talk that can be used inappropriately. Sometimes God Talk can be used to mislead others, cover sinful attitudes of the heart, or reveal a misunderstanding of God. The source of the misunderstanding could be caused by being a relatively new believer or perhaps by a conscious choice to remain "professionally weak" in faith. As we grow in our relationship with God we should naturally mature. In the maturation process we should begin to show growth in our knowledge about God and relationship with God by His Word. It is through the Bible that we are able to gain knowledge about God, His nature, and His character. It is in that knowledge we are able to use God Talk in spirit and truth.

Deceptive Hearts and the Games We Play

While the Scriptures reveal to us the nature of God and His purpose for our lives, they also tell us how deceptive our human hearts are. The Scriptures warn us not to fall for the imitations, for the substitutes from either outside sources or from hearts that are misguided and deceived. Sadly, we deceive ourselves into believing that acting Christian equates to a commitment to be a Christ-follower. To fully recognize the deceptiveness within us is extremely difficult. There are times when this deceptiveness runs deeper in our lives than we might wish to believe. It is not uncommon that this deception comes at us from unexpected sources and from unexpected directions.

It was late on Wednesday, and a normal day of counseling in my private practice was nearing an end. Receiving a call from an area Pastor-friend of mine, he requested that I see an individual as a favor to him. This last appointment was worked in as an urgent need since the Pastor was concerned for this person and felt they needed more than he was able to offer.

When she came into my office her demeanor was subdued. She introduced herself as Darlene. She was well dressed and spoke of her church as being an important part of her life; one of the larger, upper-middle-class, conservative, evangelical churches in our community.

As she began to speak a single tear formed in her eye. Her voice was soft as she told me that when she had come home the day before she had discovered a note her husband had placed on the bedside table. The note spoke of his being involved with another woman. Her husband told her it was his plan to leave her, their marriage, their three children, and that he would be soon filing for divorce. In this letter the husband went on to say that he no longer loved her and that he hoped she would recover quickly. He wished her a good future life.

This woman sitting in my office never broke down during her reporting of these recent events. Instead, in a stronger voice, she began saying things like, "God is my strength." "He is my shield." "God will provide for me and for all my needs." "God is faithful and true." "He is constant and never changing." "God is my source and my provider and will meet all the needs of my family." I was praying silently as she spoke of the recent horrible events and her faith.

Listening to her call upon the name of the Lord and recite familiar Scripture, I found myself in confusion. Let me pause here to point out that I know there are those who would turn to our loving God in the midst of trauma and tragedy finding peace at His feet. But, in my spirit as I listened to her *God Talk*, I did not feel that this was the case with this woman. I couldn't disagree with what she had said about God. She spoke all the right things. She had all the terms down pat. Her orthodoxy was accurate. However, my spirit was disquieted as I listened to her proclamations. It dawned on me that my confusion was one of whether she was passionately pursuing God or merely reciting God Talk to manipulate a horrible situation for the good according to *her* plan.

I asked her, "What are your needs?" She said, "Oh, for my husband to come home. My children need their Daddy. And, God hates divorce!" "All of that is true," I said. "But, much of what you long for will require a Godly sorrow and repentance from your husband for appropriate change to take place." "Oh no," she said. "God can make him come home and see how he has hurt us." I told her that I didn't believe that God worked in that way. Her efforts sounded manipulative to me, especially as she continued to argue her need for her husband's return. She refused to hear my words and continued to state emphatically that, "God would indeed bring her husband home." After much probing and conversation I finally stated, "I'm not sure that you can eat enough Jesus pills to make your desires come true."

Whether it was my intent or not, I had created a crisis. This Christian, petite, proper, upper-middle-class woman immediately took on the physical appearance of the Incredible Hulk. Large veins popped out from her neck as she screamed, "You can't say that to me!" "Don't you know God's Word?" "He does hate divorce, and He believes in the family!" "I thought you were a Christian counselor." As she walked through the waiting room of my office she was still yelling at the top of her voice about the un-Christian counsel she had just received.

It was probably about six weeks later when my receptionist buzzed me on the intercom and asked if I had a few moments to speak with someone. I glanced at my watch and realized I was open for the next thirty minutes or so. I opened my door and there stood Darlene. She said, "Do you remember me?" I didn't say it, but I was thinking, "Do I ever!" "How could I ever forget you?" Our last meeting was one of those unforgettable moments. Wondering what this encounter might hold, I asked her to step into my office and motioned towards a chair.

Darlene began by saying, "You were right you know." "About what?" I inquired. "About those *Jesus pills*," she said. "I tried and tried to do everything I could to talk God into bringing my husband home. I prayed harder, longer, louder, and more consistently than I ever have for anything in my entire life. What I didn't do was put my trust in God for whatever it was that He had in store for me. Your words kept haunting me. They made me mad at first, but then I began to wonder what a Jesus pill was and how that could possibly relate to me and my situation." The softness in her face let me know that she had been to the depths of despair and in that place had found relationship with her God. The peace that she possessed belied the horrible truth of what she was living. As she continued to talk she told me that her husband not only did not return, but he had moved out of state and that she had, in fact, received her divorce papers. He wasn't asking for anything but to be free from her. It was clear that she had lost her husband and the children had lost their Daddy.

I asked Darlene about the difference in her demeanor from our last meeting until now. She said that a dear friend had come to her home one day and found her exhausted from crying and near the point of a breakdown. During this visit she told her friend of our first meeting in the counseling office and what I had said to her. This friend, whom she deeply trusted and respected, told her that I was right. Darlene, at first, couldn't believe her ears. But as her conversation continued with this beloved friend she began to understand that God longed for her to pursue Him passionately, placing all her trust upon Him regardless of outcomes.

Darlene was beginning to come to an understanding. You see it's not about us being or acting Christian enough so that our lives will be comfortable and work according to our desires. It is all about Him! It is about how much He loves us and longs to give us His best for our lives.

So the question truly is: "Am I going to cooperate with God today so that my life will work?" "Or, am I going to passionately pursue God today whether my life works or not?" It is when we get to the bottom of this question by living in a passionate pursuit of God that we will find our life as God intends it. You and I were created to worship God and for that worship to be glorious.

It should be our goal to make a shift that gets us to a point in our Christian walk from mere cooperation with God to a passionate pursuit of Him.

The idea here will not always be comfortable and many times will be down right unpopular. You see if one gets serious with what the Scriptures have to say about our lives and how we should live them as we pursue relationship with God it will require both sacrifice and abandonment. The sacrifice and abandonment will be of those things that we have identified as necessary to make life work for us according to *our* ideas of what is best. Darlene is an excellent example of the point I am trying to make. Initially Darlene had a simplistic and shallow view of being in relationship with God. She was limited in her view of God and could only see Him as some indulgent grandfather willing and eager to fulfill her emotional wish list. She didn't know or understand God as the One that offers us His goodness, His love, His mercy, grace and patience, His holiness, His divine jealousy, and yes, even His wrath. God wants us to trust Him. God wants us to be *intimate* with Him! Approaching life using superficial God Talk has almost nothing to do with God. The inappropriate, superficial God Talk helps us to feel harmonious with Him but it will never lead us to intimacy with The Father. However, this misled, superficial approach is lived out daily in the lives of many Christians.

"Well Done is Better than Well Said"

If we do indeed claim Christianity as our orthodoxy (a specific practice, custom or belief; a system of ideals and values) then it becomes right and necessary that we match that orthodoxy with a supporting orthopraxis (action based on a specific practice, custom or belief; based on a system of ideals and values). This is true on many levels but for now let me just say that Jesus Himself said, "I have come to seek and save the lost." (Luke 19:10). Jesus then goes about the business of *doing* what He said He came to do. As Christ-followers we are instructed that: "As we go we are to 'make disciples.' "(Matthew 28:19, 20). It is crystal clear that when one speaks of Christianity and its values (orthodoxy) then we have to immediately recognize that these values are behavioral and must become part of our lives (orthopraxis). Sadly, many Christians already know so much more than they obey regarding God's truth and His directives about living. Why, even good ol' Benjamin Franklin stated, "Well done is better than well said."

Please don't confuse what I am saying here regarding work or works. I am not advocating the necessity of works for salvation. I am speaking of our works as being acts of worship to a Holy God who is enjoying our performance as the Supreme audience. There are those times when our sacrificial living, our heart's desire and efforts are so aligned with God that His joy cannot be contained and He applauds, as does all of heaven, with absolute joy. There are other times that would have us applauding God in our worship for His Supreme performance, Creation. In those specific times we are the audience. Our joy flows from the hope that we have and know. Our joy flows from the surety of being His. As we become overwhelmed with how He is working in our life or perhaps even in the life of someone dear to us, we explode in spontaneous applause for His work and His goodness.

Can Jealousy Ever Be Positive?

I remember years ago, back when all I had was a 9-inch amber screen Brother "word processing typewriter." At the time it was state of the art, and I felt special for having it. I remember copying something down from a *Christianity Today* magazine article and typing it into this processor; the article had to be from the early to mid 1980's. The author had a gift with his writing - what he said about marriages was something I thought to be valuable to keep on my reference shelf related to marriage. "Does the Bible Really Say All That About Romance?" was the title by a man named Rodney Clapp.   Mr. Clapp speaks to our response to God's deep and jealous love in this way:

"We have seen that love really is stronger than death, stronger than life or angels or principalities or powers or anything else (Romans 8:35-39). In the end, there is no fighting it. We already hear fiddles scratching away at a distant feast, and we wonder more and more why we ran so hard from this Lover. 'Blessed are those who are invited to the wedding supper of the Lamb!' (Revelations 19:9). We hear much of the wedding day, of great, jubilant crowds rumbling like a dozen waterfalls or rolling thunder. They have stopped running and, at long last, accepted true love. 'Alleluia!' they cry. 'Let us rejoice and be glad and give Him glory! For the wedding of the Lamb has come, and His bride has made herself ready. Fine linen, bright and clean, was given her to wear' (Revelations 19: 7, 8)."

It's true we have spent our lives running from God and His passionate, ferocious love. However, God is so perfectly consistent and so madly in love with us that He not only bears our rejection He continues to pursue us with passion. God is driven by His perfect jealousy. You see God IS the ultimate lover!

Most of the time when we use or think about the word *jealous* it strikes us as being negative in its nature. But there are times when the attribute of jealousy can be perfectly positive. "I feel a divine jealousy for you," (2 Corinthians 11:2). In this second letter to the church at Corinth the Apostle Paul expresses caring oversight for this church. Paul is speaking of protection and watch-care that is fueled by agape love.

One of the many attributes that the scriptures speak about concerning God is His divine jealousy. God is jealous for us in the way of protection for our good and for His honor. He literally commands His people not to bow down to other gods or to idols in worship. In this command He states, "for I the Lord your God am a jealous God," (Exodus 20:5). It is a true statement that our God wants us for Himself. He wants us to be in relationship with Him alone and for us not to worship the false gods that are present in our lives. The jealously that God has is for exclusivity. He is jealous for us for the purpose of protecting His own honor. That last statement will need some brief explanation.

As humans our thoughts of jealousy are believed to be selfish, especially if expressed for our own honor. Scripture is clear. Not only is there no need to protect or defend our honor we are told to be humble in our spirit. We should exhibit no pride. The reason for this directive is really very simple. You see the reason that having pride is wrong is purely theological; it is that we do not deserve the honor that belongs to God alone. "It is not wrong for God to seek His own honor, however, for He deserves it fully. God freely admits that His actions in Creation and Redemption are done for His own honor. Speaking of His decision to withhold judgment from His people, God says, 'For my own sake, for my own sake, I do it... *My glory I will not give to another,*' (Isaiah 48:11). It is healthy for us spiritually when we settle in our hearts the fact that God deserves all honor and glory from His Creation, and that it is right for Him to seek this honor. He alone is infinitely worthy of being praised. To realize this fact and to delight in it is to find the secret of true worship," (Systematic Theology, Wayne Grudem, p. 205).

We were made for the sole purpose of living in intimate relationship with God. In many cases this relationship is referred to as *knowing God.* It is so vitally important that you come to terms with the fact that our knowledge of God goes far beyond just knowing about Him. This knowledge of God should take us into the recesses of what it means to know Him and to be known by Him in intimate relationship.

It is important here that I share a tremendous quote from J.I. Packer's book *Knowing God.* This quote speaks clearly about God's ferocious love for us all and His deep desire for relationship.

"What matters supremely, therefore, is not, in the last analysis, the fact that I know God, but the larger fact which underlies it—the fact that He knows me. I am graven on the palms of His hands. I am never out of His mind. All my knowledge of Him depends on His sustained initiative in knowing me. I know Him, because He first knew me and continues to know me. He knows me as a friend, one who loves me; and there is no moment when His eye is off me, or His attention distracted from me, and no moment therefore, when His care falters.

This is momentous knowledge. There is unspeakable comfort—the sort of comfort that energizes, be it said, not enervates—in knowing that God is constantly taking knowledge of me in love, and watching over me for my good. There is tremendous relief in knowing that His love to me is utterly realistic, based at every point on prior knowledge of the worst about me, so that no discovery now can disillusion Him about me, in the way I am so often disillusioned about myself, and quench His determination to bless me. There is, certainly, great cause for humility in the thought that He sees all the twisted things about me that my fellow men do not see (and am I glad!), and that He sees more corruption in me than that which I see in myself (which, in all conscience is enough). There is, however, equally great incentive to worship and love God in the thought that, for some unfathomable reason, He wants me as His friend, and desires to be my friend, and has given His Son to die for me in order to realize this purpose. We cannot work these thoughts out here, but merely to mention them is enough to show how much it means to know, not merely that we know God, but that He knows us."

As you walk through the scriptures that follow this chapter try and center your focus on what it means – to know God! What does it mean to truly have relationship, to truly be intimate with God? If you absolutely understood that it isn't so much about having more of God, but instead a conscious effort to move towards the reality of God having more of you – what would that look like?

It is important for you and I to understand what the Scriptures have to say about this passionate pursuit of God through obedience. What is it that God requires of us? How are we to behave? How are we to speak? How are we to trust? What does it mean to be in pursuit of a Holy relationship with a loving God?

For Deeper Insight:

- When someone mentions 'The Lord's Prayer' most of us immediately take our thoughts to Matthew 6:9-13 where Jesus teaches His disciples how to pray. However, in Chapter 17 of the Gospel of John, Jesus prayed aloud to the Father several specific things just prior to allowing Himself to be arrested. Look carefully at the passage below and answer what it is that Jesus is asking the Father to grant.

- John 17:3: "Now this is eternal life: that they may know You, the only true God, and Jesus Christ, whom You have sent." (NIV).

- It is true that we were created to worship our God and that our worship is to be glorious! What evidence do we find in the Scriptures to support this idea?

- What is the theme associated with the following passages? Isaiah 43:21; Psalm 34:1; Psalm 48:1; Psalm 50:23; Psalm 63:3-8; Psalm 71:8, 14; Psalm 92:1; Psalm 96:4; Psalm 107:8; and Psalm 147:1. Why do you think this is important in the life of a Christian?

- God calls us to an 'abundant life.' What does that mean? See Ephesians 5:18-21.

- Hebrews 13:15 and 1 Peter 2:9 speak about our praises to God. How should we praise Him according to these scriptures?

- The following scriptures speak to God's character of jealousy: Exodus 20:5; Exodus 34:14; Joshua 24:19; Zechariah 1:14. There are more but for now take a look at those four references. Now think of someone or several someones who are special to you. How is it that you exhibit positive jealousy towards these individuals for protection and watch-care in agape love?

- What is it that God requires of us in our worship? See Exodus 23:25; Deuteronomy 10:12, 13; Deuteronomy 11:13-15.

- What do the following passages have to say about serving more than one master? Joshua 24:15 and Matthew 6:24

- Romans 12: 1, 2 speaks of a "living sacrifice." What does this mean? How could you become a living sacrifice for God? Would this change how you thought and behaved? How? List some of the changes.

- How is it that obedience to His Word can be seen as an act of worship?

§

Part II
Learning About Our Dance Partner
The Trinity

The Wisdom of Our GUIDE

ABBA: *Daddy, Heavenly Father*

The LAMB *and His Ferocious Love*
Part One

~ Three ~

The Wisdom of Our
GUIDE

Remember the television program *The Beverly Hillbillies?* If you watched the program, you will recall that its premise was the goofy escapades of a family from the back-wood hills that were quickly thrown into the up-scale lifestyle of the "super rich" after discovering oil on their rural farmland. "Oil, black gold, Texas tea; well, the first thing you know old Jed's a millionaire!"

In their new mansion in Beverly Hills, California, they had the advantages of many new and convenient material things that they had no idea how to utilize. "Wel-l-l doggies!" (Something Jed was famous for saying). They had all of the modern appliances but still hand-washed the dishes and the clothing, hanging the clothes on the line to dry, boiling the water for the lye soap making process, and the list goes on and on.

It was a very silly program, but it reminds me of the sad, but usual relationship between Man and the Holy Spirit in many ways. God has given us the power of His Spirit to fulfill His mission in the world, yet few Christians have even begun to depend on the beautiful gift of His indwelling power. Much like the tales of Jed Clampett and his family, we do not fully realize what it is that we possess as one of God's children, as members of His family.

Most studies of the Triune Godhead begin by speaking of God the Father, then God the Son, and finally God the Holy Spirit. Reversing this discussion sequence, I am beginning with God the Holy Spirit, and the next chapters will deal with God the Father and God the Son respectively. It is necessary to explain the Triune Godhead in this order to facilitate moving more easily into the character qualities of God the Father and Jesus Christ the Son. Approaching the study in this way will better prepare us for "The Dance."

There is some confusion on the topic of the Triune Godhead and especially this third person of the Trinity. It is not my intent or even my concern to outline the various beliefs or disagreements on the topic of the Holy Spirit. While it would be impossible to write on this subject without some theology, it is still a book dedicated to relationship with man and with God. My intent here is to emphasize the need to be in relationship while giving some general oversight to the Trinity. I'll leave the deeper insight and study about this One God who exists in Three Persons to you the reader.

I have found that many Christians spend little time gaining a deeper insight into the person of the Holy Spirit. Many are willing to live the life of Jed Clampett when it comes to embracing God the Holy Spirit in their Christian walk. I'm not exactly sure why that is the case, but I suspect it has something to do with the fact that understanding God in three persons requires time, interest, and energy. It will take time. It demands deep interest. It will require much energy in thought and study. Admittedly, this section of the book will be more intense and theological than the first section on relationships. This chapter and the next two chapters will require more thought about God in three persons: Father, Son, and Holy Spirit.

With all of that in mind let me offer a loving warning: It is here where you must pursue with diligence and with definiteness of purpose understanding for the sake of relationship building. Without a passionate pursuit you will always feel awkward on the dance floor with God. Once the three persons of the Trinity have been discussed we will focus on moving toward a deeper understanding of what will keep us from intimate relationship with God and then how to get truly comfortable as we Dance with the Trinity. Having said that let me continue with what is the focus of this chapter.

In writing about the Holy Spirit and His works I have been driven towards some new and interesting thoughts about how to explain this third person of the Trinity. Throughout my life as a Christ-follower I have either sought out older men for accountability or served in that role myself for other Christian men as they walked with God. It is in the stories of these relationships with other Christian men that I want to explain God's Holy Spirit to you.

Early on a Monday morning I was driving to a meeting - getting together with several other men. A couple of these men were relatively new to the faith and had, over the past several meetings, had some very deep and admittedly tough questions about God. While driving I began praying and asking God to give me wisdom. In fact I was asking God for His wisdom, needing Him to grant me His wisdom to help in leading these men towards a deeper relationship with Him through His Son. It was early and I was still in the process of waking up while trying to call upon God in prayer. I recall thinking how it was interesting that men always got together in the early, early hours of the morning. This of course is necessary due to our heavy work schedules as we go about the business of making a living and providing for our families. I still wished we could all meet for lunch sometimes; my bed sure felt warm as I was searching for the buzzing alarm. I don't know about you but I tend to wander somewhat during my prayer life (I believe that's fairly normal). In the midst of my wandering, God started providing for me some answers about my earlier thoughts and prayers. My spiritual alarm started to chime! I realized that I would not have been able to encourage these men and to pour God's wisdom into their life if I had not gotten up early on these many mornings. If I had not been available in relationship and had basically been an impersonal bank of information then what I desired to share would not have been readily received. I also realized that these men were important to me and that I did love them in the Lord.

In my thoughts and my prayers it began to dawn on me that is exactly what God has been doing in my life through all of these years as a Christian. I began speaking to God and saying things like: "Through Your Spirit You have become more personally involved in my life. It is through my relationship with other Christians, other members of Your Holy family, that You have taught me that I can have intimate relationship with Your Spirit. Through this experience You, God, have taught me that it is through Your Spirit that You meet me. It is through Your Holy Spirit that You have been getting up early with me and pouring Yourself into my life. It is this same Spirit that is the Spirit of Jesus, sent by Jesus to reveal and to exalt Jesus. It is His Spirit that makes our relationship wondrously intimate and delightful."

This ability to have intimate relationship with God because of His Spirit is only one of the things I have begun to realize about this third person of the Trinity. There is so much more. There is the aspect of the Spirit's comfort and His counsel. There are the times that God's Spirit serves to convict and then guide me toward holiness.

This power to be holy is a *pretty excellent* (I like that phrase) thing to behold. The power to be holy is something that can and should be deeply enjoyed. We all struggle in our efforts to move toward righteousness. Because this struggle is common among believers, we must realize that we are dead wrong when we feel that we are in this struggle alone. Yes, it's true we all struggle with the battle between the two natures. The Christians in Galatia also struggled with how to fulfill God's righteousness. The Apostle Paul wrote to the Christians in Rome about this topic as well. Here he tells the Roman Christians that God provides righteousness as a free gift in Christ (Romans 4:23-25), which a person lives out by faith (Romans 6:8-11). In Romans 7:6, 12 -14 we are reminded that God's law alone cannot change our hearts. However, the Spirit of God writes God's law in our hearts (Romans 8:2) and makes the necessary changes in our hearts to pursue God in righteousness. All of this to say, that when the Holy Spirit comes into the life of a believer He gives us an entirely new way of thinking (Romans 8: 5-6). Our hearts are changed and now we do God's will, not out of obligation, but rather because we love to please our heavenly Father in obedient worship. This obedience in love response is one that improves and develops over time. Even so, there are those times when our obedience is just that - obedience. It is done simply because we know that it is the right thing to do.

There are wonderful fruits of living in God's Spirit: love, joy, peace, patience, kindness, goodness, faithfulness, gentleness, and self-control. God's Spirit is constantly and consistently involved in advocating, encouraging, and comforting us. The Holy Spirit of God is a gift of God sent to us by the Son so that He (the Holy Spirit) can convict and secure us while, at the same time, revealing and exalting Jesus and The Father.

He is Closer to Us than We are to Ourselves

The Holy Spirit is the third person of the Trinity, who exercises the power of the Father and the Son in Creation and redemption. That is certainly a bold statement that I hope to unfold for you shortly. But, more necessary is this point: Because the Holy Spirit is the power by which believers come to Christ and see with new eyes of faith, He is closer to us than we are to ourselves. The Holy Spirit is much like the eyes of the body through which we see our physical world. We "see" our physical world through our eyes but do not view our eyes in the process. In the same way, He (the Holy Spirit - note the personal pronoun) is seldom in focus to be seen directly. Why is this? Well, it is because He is the one through who all else is seen in a "new" light. This fact alone should help you to understand why the relationship of the Father and the Son is more prominent in the gospels, because it is through the eyes of the Holy Spirit that the Father-Son relationship is viewed.

The Holy Spirit appears in the Gospel of John as the power by which Christians are brought to faith and aided in understanding their walk with God. "It is the Spirit who gives life," (John 6:63). The Holy Spirit is the Paraclete *(Counselor — one sent to assist another)*, or Helper, whom Jesus promised to the disciples after His ascension. The triune family of Father, Son, and Holy Spirit are unified in ministering to believers (John 14:16, 26). It is through the Helper that Father and Son abide with the disciples (John 15:26).

This unified ministry of the Trinity is also seen as the Spirit brings the world under conviction of sin, righteousness, and judgment. He guides believers into all truth with what He hears from the Father and the Son (John 15:26). It is a remarkable fact that each of the persons of the Trinitarian family serves the others as all defer to one another:

The Son says what He hears from the Father (John 12:49-50); the Father witnesses to and glorifies the Son (John 8:16-18, 50, 54); the Father and Son speak in their name (John 14:16, 26); the Holy Spirit honors the Father and Son by helping the community of believers.

Like Father and Son, the Holy Spirit is at the disposal of the other persons of the Triune family, and all three are one in graciously being at the disposal of the redeemed family of believers. The Holy Spirit's attitude and ministry are marked by generosity: His chief function is to illuminate Jesus' teaching, to glorify His person, and to work in the life of the individual believer and the church.

This quality of generosity is prominent in the Gospels of Matthew, Mark, and Luke, where the Holy Spirit prepares the way for the births of John the Baptist and Jesus the Son (Matt. 1:20; Luke 1:15, 35, 41). At the baptism of Jesus, the Spirit of God is present in the form of a dove. This completes the presence of the Triune family at the inauguration of the Son's ministry (Matt. 3:16-17; Mark 1:9-11; Luke 3:21-22; John 1:33). Jesus is also filled with the Holy Spirit as He is led into the wilderness to be tempted (Luke 4:1). He claims to be anointed by the Spirit of the Lord in fulfillment of Old Testament prophecy (Is. 61:1; Luke 4:18-19).

During His ministry, Jesus refers to the Spirit of God (Matt. 12:28-29; Luke 11:20) as the power by which He is casting out demons, thereby invading the stronghold of Beelzebub and freeing those held captive. Accordingly, the Spirit works with the Father and Son in realizing the redeeming power of the kingdom of God. God's kingdom is not only the reign of the Son but also the reign of the Spirit, as all share in the reign of the Father.

The person and ministry of the Holy Spirit in the Gospel is confirmed by His work in the early church. The baptism with the Holy Spirit (Acts 1:5; 2:1-4) is the pouring out of the Spirit's power in missions and evangelism (Acts 1:8). This prophecy of Jesus (and of Joel 2:28-32) begins on Pentecost (Acts 2:1-18). Many of those who hear of the finished work of God and Jesus' death and resurrection (Acts 2:32-38), repent of their sins. In this act of repentance, they receive the gift of the Holy Spirit (Acts 2:38), becoming witnesses of God's grace through the Holy Spirit.

Paul's teaching about the Holy Spirit harmonizes with the accounts of the Spirit's activity in the gospels and Acts. According to Paul, it is by the Holy Spirit that one confesses that Jesus is Lord (1 Cor. 12:3). Through the same Spirit varieties of gifts are given to the body of Christ to ensure its richness and unity (1 Cor. 12:4-27). The Holy Spirit is the way to Jesus Christ the Son (Rom. 8:11) and to the Father (Rom. 8:14-15). He is the person who bears witness to us that we are children of God (Rom. 8:16-17). He "makes intercession for us with groanings which cannot be uttered." (Rom. 8: 26-27).

The Holy Spirit also reveals to Christians the deep things of God (1 Cor. 2:10-12) and the mystery of Christ (Eph. 3:3-5). The Holy Spirit acts with God and Christ as the pledge or guarantee by which believers are sealed for the day of salvation (2 Cor. 1:21-22), and by which they walk and live (Rom 8: 3-6) and abound in hope with power (Rom 15:13). Against the lust and enmity of the flesh Paul contrasts the fruit of the Spirit: "Love, joy, peace, patience, kindness, goodness, faithfulness, gentleness and self-control." (Gal. 5:22-23).

It is the Holy Spirit that is the Power We Need to Live Life Abundantly!

As we grow in our desire to call upon and rely upon God's indwelling Spirit, we also move towards experiencing God more fully. As we yield to the majesty of the I Am, we leave the shallowness of the pursuit of harmony with God and dive head long into intimacy with our Heavenly Father. This happens when we make the conscious choice to live by the Spirit instead of pursuing a life of self-centeredness.

It should be becoming clearer that the role that God's Spirit both desires and is designed to play in our lives is ginormous. It is large beyond our imagination. However, many believers simply do not allow Him to work. The reluctance to dive into this submission is created by ignorance, fear, and sin. But I wish to encourage you to boldness. I wish to call you to the bold love of God. This requires sacrifice. This requires submission.

I Belong to God!

Before we look at the study and dig for deeper insight related to this chapter, I wish to mention one final but critical role that the Holy Spirit plays in our lives.

My life is busy. In the busyness of ministry and family it is easy for me to become wrongly focused. This wrong focus is allowing the details of life to cause me to forget the most important part of my personal identity. Were it not for the power of God's indwelling Spirit consistently praying for me and encouraging me towards the Father, I would all but lose the understanding of *Whose I am!* The Spirit of God is faithful to always remind me that I am a child of God. Regardless of whatever else God may have called me to in my life, there is no calling that is greater than the one who has beckoned me to be His child.

When life does not cooperate with us and instead makes a concerted effort to throw us its best curve balls, it is the Spirit that stands as the gentle reminder that we are God's children and that we are sealed in that relationship with Him. It is not our present circumstances but our eternal inheritance that God's Spirit reminds us of and secures us in. The gentle reminding from the Holy Spirit that we are God's children is a gift from God. This gift is both passionate and loving and is based on God's choice to draw us to relationship.

As we move to the study part of this chapter I encourage you to think about living above quiet mediocrity in your faith. By this I mean for you to consider what it would be like, even what it might look like, to step away from the usual apprehension of the Holy Spirit and give the Spirit freedom to work with power and boldness in your life. In some ways I guess it is like daring Jed to use the washing machine or dive into the cement pond. I am asking you to figure out what it would be like to enjoy relationship with God to the fullest. The Apostle Paul wrote to the church in Corinth a reprimand to stop being pulled in two different directions. He stated, "Brothers, I could not address you as spiritual but as worldly – mere infants in Christ. I gave you milk, not solid food, for you were not yet ready for it. Indeed, you are still not ready. You are still worldly. For since there is jealousy and quarreling among you, are you not worldly?" (1 Cor. 3:1-3)

The Apostle Paul has clearly divided the Corinthian Christians into two distinct and separate groups. The "worldly" Christians were obviously trying to have their cake and eat it too. They held on to God with the one hand while tightly grabbing onto the world with the other. Like the story of the rich young ruler (Luke 18:18 - 23), they wouldn't fully give their all to God. As a result of this divided effort these Christians missed out on receiving God's best. Because they were unwilling to recognize God's sovereignty and in humble submission become spiritually poor, they could only experience harmony with God, but never true intimacy.

The solution to their battle, as well as our own, between the flesh and spirit is both simple and at the same time the most difficult thing we will ever be involved with. It is surrender - surrendering to God by allowing His Spirit to lead us to the place of living under God's loving authority in obedience. We have a choice! That choice is to either gratify our sinful nature or gratify the Holy Spirit (Galatians 5:16 -17). It is impossible to do both. By gratifying the Holy Spirit we draw close to God. It is by the Holy Spirit that we come to intimacy with God. It is by living in and with the Spirit that we move into the abundant life that Christ Jesus has called us to live.

For Deeper Insight:

- The study of the Holy Spirit is of the utmost importance. Information about the Holy Spirit shared in this chapter clearly indicates that having a Scriptural understanding of God the Holy Spirit will serve to help you become a better Christ follower and will lead you to an intimate relationship with God.

- The Holy Spirit is God. He is co-equal, co-eternal, and co-existent with the Father and the Son. The Holy Spirit is also Deity.

- Take a look at the following passages: Psalm 139:7; Luke 1:35; 1 Corinthians 2:10, 11; and Hebrews 9:14. What divine attributes do these passages ascribe to the Holy Spirit?

- Read Matthew 28:19 and 2 Corinthians 13:14. Do these two passages refer to the Holy Spirit as equal to God? Why? Why not?

- If you were to do a study about Jesus Christ, God the Son, you would quickly discover how the Deity of the Holy Spirit is revealed through the life of Christ. What role did the Holy Spirit play in the life of Christ according to the following passages?

- Luke 1:35

- Acts 10:38

- Matthew 4:1

- Hebrews 9:14

- Romans 8:11

- Acts 1:2

- It is evident that Jesus depended heavily upon the Holy Spirit during His life and ministry here on earth. Can you afford to do any less?

~ Four ~

ABBA:
Daddy, Heavenly Father

I grew up on the TV shows of the mid 50's and the early 60's. One of my favorite programs was *The Art Linkletter Show*. Towards the end of his daily show he would have a segment that would feature four guest children. Mr. Linkletter would spend time speaking with each one of the children asking them seemingly innocent questions about family, God, school, growing up, etc... and their answers were absolutely hilarious. This part of the show was titled, "Kids Say the Darndest Things!"

There have been some great books written about children and many of the quotes from the Linkletter program are part of the humorous sections of those books. Awhile back I stumbled across a few questions that children asked God in letters. Let me share just a few of these wonderful quotes and ideas from children.

Dear God, Instead of letting people die and having to make new ones, why don't You just keep the ones you have now?   Jane

Dear God, It rained for our whole vacation and is my father mad! He said some things about you that people are not supposed to say, but I hope you will not hurt him anyway.   Your friend
     (but I am not going to tell you who I am).

Dear God, I think about you sometimes, even when I'm not praying.   Elliott

Dear God, I bet it is very hard for you to love all the people in the world. There are only four people in our family and I can never do it.   Nan

Dear God, Of all the people who worked for you, I like Noah and David the best.   Rob

Dear God, Maybe Cain and Abel would not kill each other so much if they had their own rooms. It works with my brother.   Larry

Dear God, I didn't think orange went with purple until I saw the sunset you made on Tuesday. That was cool!   Eugene

No wonder God wants us to come to Him as little children. There is such a refreshing simplicity about a child's conversation with God. I truly believe that we adults could learn a great deal following their transparent lead.

A child approaches God simply, expectantly, and hopefully. However, how can we mature adults approach such a vast topic as God in a simple way? While our intellect will drive us to deeper thoughts about God as an adult, our hearts should remain accepting to God in a simple manner.

Wisdom Comes From Knowing God

If God is indeed who He says He is…then any act of obedience would have to place a person in the center of His perfect Will for their life. Conversely, any act of disobedience must stem from either a willingness to ignore that God is who He says He is, or a misapprehension of the character of God. *Knowing God* i.e., relationship with Him in spirit and truth, is fundamental to all that we do.

To know God is to know what is beyond unaided human wisdom. There is tremendous value in knowing God. The heart of our spiritual warfare is against those things that oppose the knowledge of God. The vacuum created by an absence of true knowledge of God creates a vulnerability to idolatry. Furthermore, to know God is to have true knowledge. Having this true knowledge gives us the capacity to understand things as they truly are. The opposite of not knowing God is described as "folly" in the Scriptures. If a person does not seek to truly know God and to come to an understanding of His sovereignty and His holiness a person would then run the risk of opposing God (even in the midst of trying to serve Him). If a person knows God, they are then capable of standing firm with conviction even in the face of fierce opposition from a world that has learned its ways from the Prince of Lies.

To actually know God will bring a person to trusting Him in all that they say or do. It is also true that not knowing God causes a person to struggle in their day-to-day life in ways that are unnecessary and create "folly" (or perhaps the folly creates the unnecessary struggle). In the Bible it states that, "the knowledge of God is the only thing worth having." (Jeremiah 9: 23-24).

To know God results in the practice of calling upon Him. A faithful, dependant calling upon God results in knowing Him intimately. It is true that those that call upon God are those who know Him. For example: Look at the way Daniel's knowledge of God manifests itself in his prayer. Daniel did indeed call upon the Lord!

The story of Daniel in the lions' den (Daniel 6:16-28) is one of the best-known stories in the Bible. Children listen wide-eyed as their parents or Sunday School teachers first read it to them. The story is deceptively simple and uncomplicated, yet it contains some profound theological insights. It teaches that God will honor and protect those who trust and call upon Him. It also suggests that private devotional time spent with God is just as important as public worship. This is an important lesson that must not be overlooked. Many people do quite well in their faithful attendance of public worship while at the same time having no private worship time whatsoever. When our relationship with the Father is shallow we fail to recognize the importance of our personal quiet time with Him. Ultimately, the Daniel story demonstrates that a crisis reveals what kind of faith we really have. When a crisis occurs and our practice has been to regularly call upon the Father we will go to our "default" setting in faith and obedience. It is only in genuine and intimate relationship that we are able to "call upon" God.

As one gets to know God they don't somehow move into "spiritual giant-hood" or "super-spirituality." No, they become comfortable with the ordinary self and learn to drink in the encounter with a God that absolutely sees us as extraordinary. This God with His ferocious love takes hold of us, we scoundrels and ner-do-wells, and places us in the Heavenly of Heavenlies.

It seems obvious that this is where we should want to be! But, in our busyness of living and in our pharisaical approach to religion instead of relationship we have allowed the glorious, simple truth of His word to be drowned out by the pursuit of everything except Him. It is a passionate pursuit of God that is the only path to returning our hearts and our thoughts to who we really are. We are the children of God the Father. As we discover the importance of knowing God, we begin the process of relationship and "coming into our own." Our life stories will begin to testify to who our Father is. Our knowledge of God brings to us hope. Our knowledge of God helps to move us beyond harmony and brings us to intimacy with Him.

When we truly come to realize the sovereignty of God we then discover two things about ourselves that seem to be allowed to impossibly coexist. As we understand God's perfect sovereignty, we fully come to realize that any pride that we might possess has no place in the face of who He is. God is just too great. But, even in the midst of this truth, at the very same time, there exists another truth. This second truth is equally present as we come to realize the sovereignty of God. It is this second truth that functions as a road map, if you will, pointing us to a source of power that is unmatched. God is not just a resource; He is our true and ultimate source. It is through His absolute Being that we find incomprehensible power. As we humbly submit ourselves to His Lordship we are granted a power that far exceeds any human effort (2 Corinthians 12:9).

When we actually see that all things do indeed come from the hand of God and that apart from Him all things are doomed to certain failure, only then will we see our human efforts for what they are. Our GREAT accomplishments take on a "created commonness" when placed under the eyeglasses of a sovereign God (a paraphrase of Francis Schaeffer).

At the same time our commonness is utterly exposed, we discover that we have the attention, the listening ear of the One who is the "I AM" and who "….even the wind and the waves obey." (Mark 4:41). The encouragement to all is to seek this One first, to ask of this One, to knock upon His door and receive. As we approach His throne in humbleness He promises to lift us up.

What perfect power! Who is this God who holds the entire universe securely and by His Will? Who is this Sovereign Lord who keeps all we know and beyond of this universe in motion? One cannot even begin to imagine that this God places His power and presence into every atom, particle and microscopic piece of the whole - everything. The thought of this in its totality is just too great. Father God knows each of His children by name, counts the stars and the grains of sand, and cares for the sparrow. What kind of God is this who can endow the crown of His creation with free will and still maintain constant and perfect control over the events and flow of history?

While there are many, many names used for this God, The Sovereign may perhaps be most fitting. He is the sovereign One and His ongoing relationship with the world is one of *complete sovereignty.*

This idea of sovereignty is one that is basically hard to swallow. This is especially true in our American culture that prides itself on independence (an attribute of God's, not us). Even professing believers struggle with ideas, terms, even movements of autonomy, rebellion, and liberation. The idea of sovereignty is scary and difficult because it can best be defined or summed up as *absolute Lordship.* The problem with grasping and accepting the principle of a sovereign God is that it forces us to yield to His absolute Lordship simultaneously. The term Lord directly speaks to ownership. If God is sovereign then He has absolute Lordship and thus is absolute owner of all. In other words, to say that God is sovereign means that he is Lord in the sense of the owner of all things.

The scriptures testify to His Lordship. Melchizedek and Abraham refer to Him as "possessor of heaven and earth," (Gen. 14:19, 22). Moses says, "Behold, to the Lord your God belong heaven and the highest heavens, the earth and all that is in it," (Deut. 10:14). Psalm 24:1 echoes this: "The earth is the Lord's, and all it contains, the world, and those who dwell in it." "All the earth is Mine," says the Lord (Exod. 19:5). "Whatever is under the whole heaven is Mine," (Job 41:11).

There is one more point that I wish to make about His absolute Lordship, i.e. sovereignty: *It goes far beyond just mere ownership.* God is ruler, has dominion over, kingship and royal power in and over all. Furthermore, the Lordship is absolute in the sense that it is eternal. Jeremiah 10:10 states, He is "the everlasting King, the King eternal."

The Bible reveals God as the only Infinite and Eternal Being (eternity past and eternity future), having no beginning and no ending. He is Creator and Sustainer of all things. He is the Supreme Personal Intelligence and Righteous Ruler of His universe. He is life, and therefore, the only source of life (John 5:26).

Man (mankind) is natural and cannot know God by wisdom. While our wisdom is helpful in understanding things about God, wisdom cannot bring us to a point of knowing God in relationship. "Can you discover the depths of God?" (Job 11:7).

God is a person and can be known only by revelation. It is in the passionate pursuit of God in relationship that He [God] reveals Himself to the one that diligently searches for Him. It is the one who pursues God in relationship that is blessed by God's revelation in love. In the Old Testament He revealed Himself to and through His prophets. In the New Testament He reveals Himself through His Son Jesus Christ (Heb 11:5, 6).

There are many things that could be studied concerning The Eternal God, i.e., the Personality of God, the Righteousness of God, His Providence, God's Miracles, the Sovereignty of God, the Trinity of God, and we could even study the "Know-ability" of God, etc... However, I want to focus on just three aspects of God. For the study part of this chapter, I want us to look briefly at God's Existence, God's Grace, and God's Nature.

For Deeper Insight:

God's Existence

- The Existence of God is an interesting topic. It is interesting because the Bible nowhere attempts to prove or argue the existence of God. All persons everywhere have a deep, inner sense that God exists, that they are His creatures, and that He is their Creator. Paul says that even Gentile unbelievers "knew God" but did not honor Him as God or give thanks to Him (Romans 1:21). There is an assumption to God's existence from the rational intuition of man in the Scriptures. We are called upon to believe in God through faith. Let me explain:

- The existence of God is a fact that is taken for granted by the writers of both the Old and the New Testaments. "In the beginning God..." (Gen 1:1 OT). The Bible opens by announcing the sublime fact of God and His existence.

- I believe as we look at some scriptures about faith we will come to understand why the Bible has taken a "cause and effect" approach to helping man believe in God.

- Take a look at the passage in Hebrews 11:5–6. What do you think it means when it says: "For he who comes to God must believe that He is...?"

Faith

- Faith is: the assurance (title deed) of things hoped for. Your faith is your title deed to eternal life. Just as a title deed is evidence of real estate, so your faith is evidence of your eternal estate in God. Turn to 2 Corinthians 4:18 and think about what it means to focus on the things that are not seen.

- Faith is: taking God at His word and asking no questions. What reward did Enoch receive by purely believing in God in Hebrews 11:5–6?

- Faith is: knowing that "God causes all things to work together for good" (Romans 8:28). Is this passage saying all things are good and work well or is it saying all things (good or bad) work together for good to those who love God?

- Faith has two sides: One side of faith has to do with our intellect. It is through an intellectual conviction that Jesus Christ is God. (We will look at this deeper in the next

chapter). The other side of faith has to do with our will.
Through faith we harness our will's to do the Will of God.
This is a voluntary surrender. It is done volitionally in
direct proportion to the faith that we have. Look at the
following Scriptures: John 20:28; John 20:31. What do
these scriptures reveal about an intellectual conviction and
a volitional surrender?

- Faith is paradoxical. For the reasonable man, faith goes
  beyond reason. Faith believes without understanding why.
  It is by faith that one would praise and bless God in times
  of trouble. By faith the prisoner can sing. And, it is by faith
  that we learn to accept all things as part of God's perfect
  plan. Take a look at the following scriptures: Acts 16:25;
  Hebrews 11:25; Philippians 1:12; Romans 10:17; Romans
  10:13–14. What do these specific passages say about faith?
  How do they say that faith is obtained?

When is your inner sense of God's existence the
strongest? When is it at its weakest? Why? In which of these
two situations are your judgments more reliable? Why do you
believe this?

God's Grace

Simply put Grace is getting what one does NOT deserve
to have. Adrian Rodgers said one day from his pulpit that Grace
should be understood in this way: **G**od's **R**iches **A**t **C**hrist's
Expense. Grace is the love and mercy of God in action. To
show mercy in love is grace. God showed mercy in love when
He sent His Son to bear our sins in His own body on the cross
(John 3:16).

- What does Romans 8:38–39 say about the way that God's
  grace saves?

- Take a look at the following passages of scripture and list some of the various characteristics and qualities of God's perfect grace: 2 Corinthians 12:9; Revelation 22:17; Romans 3:23–24; Titus 3:7; Titus 2: 11–12. After listing the qualities and characteristics of grace write down a summary statement about what the grace of God has done for you.

- The grace of God is nothing less than the unlimited love of God expressed in the gift of His Son, our Savior. It is the undeserved love of God towards you and I – sinners.

Why do you think that some people deny the existence of God? What does Romans 1:18 suggest might contribute to their intellectual denial of God's existence (cf. Psalm 14:1–3)?

In Isaiah 6:3 it states that the seraphim around God's throne cried out, "Holy, holy, holy is the Lord of Hosts; the whole earth is full of His glory." Is it possible for us to praise God in this way, right now, as we live on this earth? Why? Why not? How would/could we do this?

God's Nature

There are four definitions of God in the Bible. This is a funny statement in that God cannot be defined. So, obviously these definitions are incomplete. However, these four descriptions or definitions will serve to shed some light on the Nature of God and thus are important for us to look at.

Look at the following passages: 1 John 4:8; 1 John 1:5; Hebrews 12:29; and John 4:24. What do these passages say about the Nature of God? Make a list.

You can also discover things about God's Nature by looking at attributes that are ascribed to God in the Scriptures. Study the following verses. What attributes are given to God in these passages? John 5:26; Psalm 147:5; Revelation 19:6; and Psalm 139:1–10. List these attributes on a piece of paper. Think about these deeply (meditate). Ask God to reveal Himself to you as you seek to know Him fully.

Lastly, God is everywhere present, but He is not in everything. If this were true, that God is in everything, man could worship any object and he would be worshiping God. God is a spirit being. Those that long to worship Him must worship the one true God in spirit and truth.

~ Five ~

The LAMB
and His Ferocious Love

Part One

There are two groups of people that I will admit showing a level of favoritism towards. The first group is F.A.T. adults. By that I mean Faithful, Available, and Teachable. People within this group seem to have a zest for life and for learning. They ask the poignant and interesting questions. These people serve to stimulate great and meaningful conversation. They long to know more about most everything. It is especially rewarding for me to be involved with a member of this particular brand of people in thought provoking conversation about things of God. It is in these conversations where "God Talk" is rich, sweet, and serves to drive the participants to the depths of life and its meaning. When I am involved in those types of conversations with F.A.T. adults I feel a level of satisfaction that I find in few other places in my life.

Now, the second category of people I find most interesting are those that fall into the group called four-year-olds. These guys are absolutely fabulous! They have survived the toddler stage and lost most of their baby traits. These little folks are beginning to come into their own as individuals. It is around this age that their individual personalities begin to obviously shine. When they are excited about something and long to share their excitement their expressions are priceless. Their eyes widen, their speech becomes rapid, and they repeat many times what they are trying to tell you about. They are overwhelmed in their simple exuberance about life. These little folks become completely immersed in the story they are trying to share. The excitement in their lives is contagious and positive. I will admit to hanging out with this group whenever possible. I believe it was four-year-olds that Jesus was speaking about when he said, "Truly, I say to you, unless you turn and become like children, you will never enter the kingdom of heaven," (Matthew 18:3). These guys love the world around them and are excited to be a part of it.

I remember several years ago doing some volunteer work with the 4-year-old class at a Sunday School. I had been asked to teach the lesson for that Sunday taken from the Book of James, Chapter 4 and verse 8. In this verse it simply states, *"Draw near to God and He will draw near to you..."* One of the young students of the class came to me at the end of class and wanted to declare her understanding of the day's lesson. She tugged on my shirt and motioned for me to bend down. When I got to her level she said, "If you color next to Jesus, He will color next to you." While she didn't have the lesson exactly right, I'm not so sure that she missed the meaning of what was being taught that day.

That afternoon I went home, turned on the television and started watching a Sunday afternoon football game. As I watched the game it dawned on me that Jesus would probably love to "pull up a floor" with me and enjoy the game. Jesus loved people and wanted all to understand the deep love that He held for them. If watching the game on television was important to me, then it would take on a certain level of importance for my Savior as well. Jesus always seemed to be willing to meet people exactly where they were. In doing so He spent time with them in their place while encouraging them to move towards Him. He longed for each person to know the absolute depth of His love. It really is true that if I "color next to Jesus then He will absolutely love coloring next to me!"

Jesus wants us to have relationship with Him and with the Father through Him. God the Father created us for His good pleasure. We were created for relationship. In that relationship we are to worship God, and our worship should be glorious.

Alas, Man failed and eternally altered his ability to stay in "right" relationship with God. But, in His deep, faithfully consistent and abiding love God still desperately longed to be with His children. It was the sin of Man that was the ultimate cause that led to Christ's coming to earth and dying for me and for you. Christ's death was absolutely necessary because of the nature and character of God. It was because of God's perfect love and His perfect justice that Christ's death of Atonement was required.

God's love is clearly seen in John 3:16 where it states, *"For God so loved the world that He gave His only begotten Son, that whoever believes in Him should not perish but have eternal life."* But, the justice of God also required that God find a way that the penalty due to us for our sins would be paid (God could not accept us into fellowship with Him unless the penalty for sin had been paid in full).

How Can Jesus Be Fully God and Fully Man at the Same Time?

I guess the best place to begin a discussion about Jesus Christ would be to ask what is probably the most obvious question of all. How is it that Jesus can be fully God and at the same time be fully man? How is it that this Jesus can be both, yet is one person?

Christianity differs from all other religions, because it is more than just a religion. Christianity is the life of the Son of God made living in man. Christ IS Christianity, and Christianity IS Christ.

The One Who Holds the Universe Together has come down to live with us. This Divinity arrived and for the most part his arrival and life went unnoticed. He came down to serve us and to show us how to live. Jesus, the Christ, the Son of the Living God came to earth in humble and holy submission to the Will of the Father. In his submissive, servant's spirit Jesus died for us - God incarnate, *Immanuel*, or God with us. You might not realize this but the Word of God does not use the term *incarnation* anywhere in its pages to refer to the fact that Jesus was God in human flesh. This "incarnation" was the act of God the Son. In this deliberate act Christ took upon Himself the nature of a human.

Throughout all of Scripture it is the person of Christ Jesus that is the topic. It is the person of Christ Jesus that is the theme. He is the supreme subject of each and every book of the New Testament, and He [Christ] fulfills all the promises of God in the Old Testament. You will come to a much fuller realization of this in the Appendix: The Names and Titles of Jesus (Part Two on The LAMB)*. According to both the Book of Genesis and the Gospel of John, Jesus has been since and before, "In the beginning!" Jesus is the manifestation of God's promises from His incarnation to His Second Coming as "Lord of lords and King of kings," (Revelation 17:14).

The Humanity of Christ is a topic that commands some conversation if we are to understand whom the Son of God actually is. When we speak of the humanity of Christ it is both important and appropriate to begin with a brief discussion of the virgin birth of Christ. The Gospel of Luke clearly asserts that Jesus was to be conceived in the womb of his mother Mary by a miraculous work of the Holy Spirit and without a human father.

> "The Holy Spirit will come upon you, and the power
> of the Most High will overshadow you; therefore
> the child to be born will be called holy, the Son of
> God," (Luke 1:35; cf3:23).

There are three areas of extreme importance concerning the Christian doctrine of the virgin birth of Jesus Christ. It is not the effort of this book, much less this chapter, to be an exhaustive systematic approach to deep understandings of the things of God, the Son, or the Holy Spirit. It is more important that significant ideas be introduced and that you be encouraged to dig deeper into the scriptures for personal answers to the significant questions of the Christian faith.

Having said that, let's look at these three important points surrounding the virgin birth and the humanity of Christ:

1. The virgin birth: shows that salvation ultimately must come from the Lord. Just as God had promised that the "seed" of the woman (Genesis 3:15) would ultimately destroy the serpent, so God brought it about by His own

power, not through mere human effort. This is such an important point for us to remember that our salvation only comes about through the supernatural work of God not through any work of our own.

2.   The virgin birth: made possible the uniting of full deity and full humanity in one person. It was through this means that God used to send His "only begotten Son," (John 3:16). Think about those words "only begotten" because they are centrally important. If a hippo or a horse begets an offspring they would beget their own kind – a hippo or a horse. If God begets then it is true that God begets His own kind. God begets God. This virgin birth was the means that God used to send His Son to earth as a man. With a little time and some creative thought one would likely be able to generate other ways that Christ could have come to earth. Some might assert, and I guess it could have happened in this way, that God might have chosen to have created Jesus as a man and then sent Him to earth. However, if that had been God's elected approach it would have been very difficult for us to see how Jesus could be fully human as we are (Hebrews 4:15). Also, there would be equal difficulty in viewing or accepting Jesus as a true part of our human race and as a descendent from Adam. It is through this virgin birth that Christ's humanity would be evident to us from the fact of His ordinary human birth, and at the same time His full deity would be evident due to His conception in Mary's womb by the powerful work of God's Holy Spirit.

3.   The virgin birth: makes possible Christ's true humanity without inherited sin. The fact that Jesus did not have a

human father shows that the line of descent from Adam is partially interrupted. This interruption removes from Christ Jesus the legal guilt and moral corruption that belongs to all other human beings.

The Christian doctrine of the virgin birth is central to understanding the ideas and concepts associated with the humanity of Christ Jesus. You must also realize that His virgin birth, His holy, sinless life, His many miracles, and His vicarious death and His bodily resurrection all point to His deity as well.

During His earthy ministry, Jesus claimed to be God incarnate (in human flesh). I love what Josh McDowell has to say in his book *More Than a Carpenter*. Just the title of his third chapter says it all: "Lord, lunatic or liar?" You see the point that Josh McDowell is trying to make here is that Jesus the Christ is either all that He claimed to be, or He is less than the least.

I absolutely love it when I get into a conversation with someone who tries to be politically correct about this man called Jesus. Somewhere in our conversation this "PC" individual will say something like: *While I can't go so far as to believe that your Jesus is God, I will have to admit that he was an excellent teacher. The ideas he shared about getting along and loving people are important for all of us.*

Statements like the one I just shared are from someone who engaged their mouth long before turning on their brain. It is obvious that they either haven't considered or perhaps do not know what Jesus actually taught. There is not time to pull out all of the Scriptures that record the teachings of Jesus, our Lord and Savior. However, I would encourage you to make that a particular study of yours after finishing this book. But, I do want to look at just one of His radical claims.

There is one particular passage found in Revelation 1 verse 8 that commands an answer to the argument of whether or not Christ Jesus is actually who He claims to be. In this passage Jesus says the following: "I am the Alpha and the Omega, who is and who was and who is to come, the Almighty." Not a lot a gray area in that statement, huh?

That statement is indeed a powerful and daunting proclamation by our Savior. There are many, many other similar statements that Christ made about Himself. But, don't take my word for it – dig deep, study. Answer for yourself if He is the Savior. If He is not, then one must also reject the idea that He was a good teacher.

There is one key factor that allows Jesus alone to make the claim that He is the Almighty. The fact of His sinless nature is what differentiates Him from every other human. Though the New Testament clearly affirms that Jesus was fully human just as we are, it also affirms that He was sinless (*see* Hebrews 4:15). Jesus Christ had no sin, knew no sin, thought no sin and being sinless could live as no man has ever lived, before or since. Some might argue that if Jesus did not sin, then he was not truly human. That argument would be based on the Scriptural reference that *all [humans] have sinned* (Romans 5:12). But, should you fall into that camp or align with that argument let me remind you that God did not create us sinful, but holy and righteous. Adam and Eve in the Garden before they sinned were truly human, and we now, though human, do not match the pattern that God intends for us when our full, sinless humanity is restored.

Jesus Referred to Himself as God

It is equally important for me to spend some time discussing the deity of Christ. You see not only do we need to understand the humanity of Christ, but we must also come to a deeper understanding of His deity as well.

Others referred to Jesus as God, and Jesus referred to Himself as God. The word God (Theos) is used many times in the New Testament to refer to Jesus Christ. While this word is usually reserved for referring to God the Father the several passages that use this to mean Christ Jesus are clear in their meaning and show Christ's deity. Some of the passages are as follows: John1:1; 1:18; 20:28; Romans 9:5; Titus 2:13; Hebrews 1:8 (this is a quote from Psalm 45:6); and 2 Peter 1:1 to name a few.

One clear example when Christ refers to Himself as God is found in the Book of John 8:57. Here Jesus told His Jewish opponents that Abraham had seen His [Christ's] day. This absolutely infuriated the crowd and drove them to a direct challenge by saying, "You are not yet fifty years old, and have you seen Abraham?" Jesus' response to their angry assertions was, "Truly, truly, I say to you, before Abraham was, I AM," (John 8:58). This statement by Jesus put all the cards on the table as far as the Jewish leaders were concerned. By referring to Himself as "I AM" He was repeating the very words God used when He identified Himself to Moses, "I Am Who I AM," (Exodus 3:14). It is here that Jesus is claiming for Himself a title that is God. With this name, I Am, He is stating His eternality, He is stating He is One with the Father, He was claiming to be God.

In the previous chapter (ABBA) I referred to the passage of scripture found in Mark 4:41. I realized that the reference there is specifically to Christ the Son of God, but I chose to use that to emphasize the 'Oneness' of the Triune Godhead. It was my effort to highlight that the Father and the Son are One and that if one *"has seen me [Christ] they have seen the Father,"* (John 14:9).

Jesus shows His deity in many ways throughout His earthly ministry. He demonstrated His *omnipotence* when He performed the miracle of quieting the storm and stilling the seas that generated the response of the disciples referenced in Mark 4:41. His first of many earthly miracles was at the wedding in Cana of Galilee. There, Jesus turned the water into wine (John 2:1 – 11). He showed His reign over the natural by multiplying the loaves and fish (Matthew 14:19). At the wedding feast upon seeing His miracle the disciples believed upon Him; in the storm the disciples marveled and wondered, "…who is this that even the winds and waves obey?"

Jesus too possessed divine sovereignty. This kind of absolute authority is reserved for God and God alone. Jesus reveals His sovereignty by forgiving sins (Mark 2:5–7). In another way of revealing His divine sovereignty Jesus spoke differently than the Old Testament prophets when acting on "behalf" of God. When the prophets would speak they would always proclaim, thus said the Lord. However, when Jesus spoke He could preface His statements with, "But, I say to you…," (Matthew 5:22, 28, 32, 34, 39, 44). It is here in His Sermon on the Mount where Jesus boldly proclaims His own authority.

Jesus is the Good News!

I have often wondered how great it would be to have had the opportunity, as Adam and Eve had, to have walked with God. God would come to the Garden and speak to Adam and discuss the workings of His Creation. Adam was allowed to participate in the naming of the lesser members of the animal kingdom. Adam, as the first man, had what could only be defined as an absolutely unique relationship with the Lord. To say the difference in "Man's" relationship before and after the Fall is astounding is certainly stating the obvious. Once able to walk and talk with God, the post-Fall Man could only hide his face in absolute shame and nakedness.

The non-believer wonders what is so good about the Good News. Well, the answer is simple. Stop for a brief moment and truly think about what happened when Man fell in Sin. All that was known in Creation was lost. The Garden was a place that possessed beauty beyond description prior to the Fall of Man. All of Nature existed in perfect harmony. The waters were clear and without pollution, the flora was fragrant, and the foliage was thick and rich with color and life. After the Fall, death, destruction, and decay entered Creation. The putrid smell of rot now hovers where sweetness once existed and purity was in abundance. The ability to "dance" in the fullness of relationship was lost and could not be recovered without God's intervention. However, since that horrible event in the history of mankind, God has been about the business of bringing us back into relationship with Himself. He has done this through the unexplainable love that He has shown through the sacrificial death of His Son, Christ Jesus as a propitiation for our sins. It was the work at the Cross done in a spirit of obedience by God's only begotten Son that has made a way for me, for you, for all who have sinned to have the ability to be in relationship with God. It is because of this act, and this act alone, that God calls man unto Himself. So you see the "good news" [Gospel] is salvation from sin. This Gospel is the revelation of God's grace in the death and resurrection of Jesus Christ and the possibility of new life through faith in Him. In this new life of faith in Him, God instructs man to be transformed by the "renewing of your mind" (Romans 12: 1- 4). He calls us to repent and be saved. God calls us to seek forgiveness, and we will be forgiven. God longs to have relationship with us and has shown us that no cost is too great in order to make a way for that relationship to occur.

Many of you might be familiar with steps to salvation described as the Roman-road. In case you are not let me lay it out for you in this chapter:

God's Four Steps To Salvation

Step 1: Recognizing God's Desire For Us To Experience An Abundant Life

God loves you and desires that you experience joy, peace, and the abundant life. This life is in God's only begotten Son, Jesus Christ Our Lord!

The Bible Says....

John 3:16 For God so loved the world, that He gave His only begotten Son, that whosoever believes in Him should not perish but have everlasting life.

John 11:25 Jesus said to her, I am the resurrection, and the life; he who believes in me lives even if he dies.

John 10:10 …I came that they might have life, and might have it more abundantly.

What keeps most people from experiencing the joy, peace, and the abundant life that God has planned for them?

Step 2: Recognizing Man's Problem: Separation From God!

God created man in His own image and made him a free mortal agent. God didn't want robots worshiping him but gave them freedom of choice. Man made the choice to disobey God. Man's rebellion against God is called sin. Man then is a sinner by will and freedom of choice.

Man willfully chose to disobey God and go his own selfish ways! Man still makes this choice today. This results in separation from God and an eternal life in Hell!

The Bible Says...

Romans 3:23 For all have sinned and fall short of the Glory of God.

Romans 6:23 For the wages of sin is death; but the free gift of God is eternal life through Jesus Christ our Lord.

Man through the years has tried to bridge this gap without success...

There is only one Solution (Soul-ution) to this Problem of Separation.

Step 3: Recognizing God's Solution:
The Cross!

Our Lord Jesus Christ is the only solution to this problem of separation from God.

When our Lord Jesus Christ died on the cross, He paid the penalty for all our sins and bridged the gap from God to man.

The Bible Says...

Romans 5:8 But God demonstrates His own love toward us, in that while we were yet sinners, Christ died for us.

John 14:6 Jesus said to him, I am the way, and the truth, and the life: No one comes to the Father, but by me.

Ephesians 2:8, 9 For by grace you have been saved through faith; and that not of yourselves, it is the gift of God; not as a result of works, that no one should boast.

God has provided in Jesus Christ the only way of salvation... Man must make the choice to receive God's solution.

Step 4: Man's Response:
To Receive Christ As Personal Savior

We all must trust in The Lord Jesus Christ! We must receive Him into our hearts by inviting him into our hearts personally.

The Bible Says...

Revelation 3:20 Behold I stand at the door and knock: if anyone hears My voice and opens the door, I will come in to him, and will dine with him, and he with Me.

John 1:12 But as many as received Him, to them He gave the right to become children of God even to those who believe in His name.

Romans 10:13 ...for "Whoever will call upon the name of the Lord will be saved."

Is there any good reason why you cannot receive Jesus Christ as your own personal Lord and Savior?

What Must You Do?

1. Admit your need (I am a Sinner)

2. Be willing to turn from sin (Repent)

3. Believe that Jesus Christ died for you (On the Cross)

4. Through prayer, receive Him as your personal Lord and Savior

A Suggested Prayer of Commitment: Dear Father God, I know that I am a sinner and need your forgiveness. I believe that Your Son Jesus Christ died in my place, paying the penalty for all my sins. I am willing to turn away from sin. I now invite Jesus Christ to come into my heart and life as my own personal Savior. I am willing with your help to follow and obey Jesus Christ as the Lord of my life! Amen

What's Next?

1. Pray Daily

2. Read The Bible Daily! (Start off with reading the Book of John.)

3. Go to a good Bible-preaching Church where they teach God's Word!

4. In obedience follow this decision with the act of baptism according to the Scriptures.

5. Tell others about the decision you made!

6. Tell others about the Good News that Jesus Christ can save them!

Some of you might truly wonder why I took the time to lay out the entire Roman-road to Salvation here in this book. Actually there are a couple of reasons: First, as we mature in our faith our goal will become modeling Christ as we Dance with the Trinity. In our dance we grow to the point that our deepest desire is to present every man mature in Christ. I will develop this point later in chapter eight. But, it is important that you have this tool to utilize as you develop relationships with people that express an interest in knowing how to become saved through Christ Jesus. Secondly, I know in my heart that it is at this point someone has just received Christ as their personal Lord and their personal Savior as a result of what they have just read. It is for that one person that I have written this last section.

Now the question then becomes this... If I have come to God through the saving work of Christ Jesus, then what must I do to position myself in such a way as to put myself in the center of God's perfect Will for my life? How would one go about being transformed? What ways would I pursue to renew my mind? How can I ready myself for "The Dance?" We will answer all of these questions in later chapters. But, for now let's focus on the Scriptures and what they have to say about Jesus the Son of God.

As we approach the study part of this chapter I want us to focus on three important aspects of Jesus. First, I want to look at His deity as described in the Scriptures; second, I would like to study the Resurrection of Jesus; and, third, I would like to dig deeper into the Ascension and Second Coming of the Christ.

For Deeper Insight:

The Deity Of Christ

- The deity of Jesus Christ, or His God nature, is well established in the New Testament. God Himself refers to the Son as God. The Apostles recognize Jesus as God. And, Jesus proclaims that He is One with the Father, thus God.

- Take a look at the following passages in the Gospel of John: John 1:1; 8:51–59; 17:5; and 20:28. Now look at Hebrews 1:8. What do these passages say about Jesus?

- Is it appropriate to worship Jesus as God? Look at: Matthew 14:33. What does this tell you about how we are to worship Jesus? Take a look at Revelation 22:8, 9; and Acts 10:25; 26. What do these two passages tell you about how Jesus compares with angels and with man?

- What does Mark 2:5–11 tell you Jesus is capable of?

- For what does Colossians 1:16 tell you that Jesus is responsible?

- What does Hebrews 1:3 say that Jesus does?

- In Matthew 28:18 Jesus claims what?

- About the deity of Christ: He walked upon water; the winds and the waves obeyed His command; He healed the sick; raised the dead; gave sight to the blind; and gave hearing to the deaf. Jesus cast out demons and made lame people able to walk. Jesus turned water into wine and fed five thousand with a small boy's lunch. Jesus is God!

The Resurrection Of Christ

First take a look at Matthew 28:1–20.

- The resurrection of Christ was and is the doctrine of every disciple, the faith of every true believer, the courage of every martyr, the theme of every sermon, and the power of every effort of evangelism. What did Jesus say about this topic according to John 11:25?

- How is it possible to prove the resurrection of Christ? Were there any eye-witnesses to His resurrection? If so, who are they?

- Look at: John 20:11–18; Matthew 28:5–10; Luke 24:34; 24:13–31; 24: 36–43; John 20: 24–29; 21: 1–23; 1 Corinthians 15:6; 15:7; Matthew 28:16–20; Acts 1:3–12; 7:55; 9:3–6; 1 Corinthians 15:8.

- Make a list of the witnesses and their response to seeing Jesus.

The Ascension And Second Coming Of Christ

- What does Acts 1:9–11 tell you about Christ's Ascension into Heaven?

- Now that Christ has ascended where is He? Look at Hebrews 10:12.

- The message of the second coming of Jesus is so important that it is mentioned over three hundred times in the New Testament.

- Why is Jesus coming back? Take a look at the following passages and list as many reasons as you can as to why Jesus will be returning to earth again one day: 1Thessalonians 4:16, 17; John 14:1–6; Matthew 25:31–46; Romans 11:25, 26; Luke 1:31-33. Also see Isaiah 9: 6, 7; Hebrews 1:8; and Revelation 22:20.

* Appendix: The LAMB and His Ferocious Love - Part Two

§

Part III
Preparing For the Dance

**Barriers to Healthy Relationships
and Dancing Gracefully**

Dance Lessons that Lead to Obedience

The Dance

**Appendix
The LAMB *and His Ferocious Love***
Part Two

~ Six ~

Barriers to Healthy
Relationships
and Dancing Gracefully

W e do indeed have a formidable dance partner. The preceding chapters (both the reading and studies) present a clear picture of a Holy God of love, passion, and pursuit. There is only one true God. This one true God has revealed Himself as a "Trinity" of three Persons: Father, Son, and Holy Spirit. Each of these three persons is truly, fully, and equally God. The Bible speaks of the glory of God the Father; it says that the Word (Jesus Christ) was God; and it speaks of the Lord, who is the Spirit. There is only one God, but there are three Persons in the Godhead.

We have been fearfully and wonderfully made by God, who loves us dearly. The Scriptures are clear about God having created us. The Scriptures are also clear on His ordaining our days before the foundations of Creation. God has a plan for us and our individual stories are woven into His overall plan for humanity and Creation.

While it is true that we have all been created in the image of God, we are at the same time all uniquely different. Our differences are part of what it means to be created in the image of God. Sameness is an affront to a God that is a creative genius. If it weren't for our differences from one another the world would be infinitely boring. In many respects we are all thankful for the differences that we have from those around us. However, it is in these differences that our problems with relationship occur.

When we look at these differences we tend to evaluate and give value to the various points of view. Because of our sin nature we tend to support our individual ideas and views as being right, or at least more right, than others. It is through this sin nature that we exhibit our individual pride and selfishness. Our pride and our selfishness are the base cause for the destruction of relationship with one another and with God. In our relationships we frequently yield to our sin nature and exhibit wrong behaviors. Our wrong choices lead us to lie, to cheat, hide from the truth, to bear false witness, and the list goes on and on. The sins of pride and selfishness exist as we work to gratify our flesh. As we pursue this path for our lives we fail to follow God's directives. In choosing the sinful path instead of the path of obedience we lose intimacy with God and with our fellow man. Only God knows our heart and frankly His opinion of Man's heart is not very good. I want to develop that thought just a little as it relates to relationships and our pride in this chapter.

The Easy Way Out

Throughout the early years of my life my Father told me that things worth having usually require hard work. He knew the value of sweat equity and taught me the valuable principle of taking pride in what I was doing. My Father taught me to work hard and to do the very best I could in any endeavor. If I heard it once I heard it a million times: "Do the right thing and do the right thing well," (a statement that my children would say they have heard far too many times in their lives). Hard work is not a popular idea. The idea of hard work in relationship is even less popular because it is not rightly understood.

People tend to approach relationships the way they approach financial planning. Everyone desires an impressive financial portfolio, but few people take the necessary steps in planning and long-term investing with proven, sound principles to realize this desire. It is more common that one just dreams of winning the lottery and being set for life! The idea of fiscal discipline is foreign and unattractive. So it is in relationship.

True intimacy in relationship requires risk and discipline. The risk and discipline come in the forms of humility and obedient submission to His lordship as we shape our lives into living sacrifices that are both holy and pleasing to our God. As stated in an earlier chapter, "if one gets serious with what the Scriptures have to say about our lives and how we should live them as we pursue relationship with God and with one another, it will require both sacrifice and abandonment. The sacrifice and abandonment will be of those things that we have identified as necessary to make life work for us according to our ideas of what is best." Herein lies the rub. We want relationship. We want to have and experience relationship abundantly. We are not willing to shape our lives to become obedient to God and His plan to experience relationship to its fullest. Like the lottery winner we want our wealth, and we want it now without the necessary sweat equity. We want all of the benefits that come from knowing God and living obediently without truly being obedient. We desire the benefits without truly being disciplined in our humble pursuit of God.

Pride, the Main Tool in Satan's Vast Arsenal:
Pride Leads to an Unforgiving Spirit

I remember a time in my life when I clearly decided to do something for someone for the sole purpose of ministry and making their life easier. It wasn't a really difficult thing for me to do and initially I started out feeling blessed for being able to serve this person in such a small but specific way. It was about the fourth month of my serving this person that I began to recognize a shift in my attitude about what I had set out to do. I found that I was developing feelings of resentment towards this person because they had not taken the time to notice how I had been attempting to serve them. As I mulled over their lack of gratitude I became more and more resentful. It wasn't long before feelings of anger and bitterness were welling up from within instead of the initial blessed feelings of service and ministry.

Funny how it works - isn't it? I started out with this altruistic desire to minister, to serve, to glorify God with my behavior. Before I knew it I was filled with resentment and bitterness because I wasn't getting my well-deserved pat on the back.

What caused the change in my thought, the change in my attitude? Why had I moved from what was good and right to what was wrong and selfish? How had this demanding spirit developed so quickly? How had this demanding spirit developed so easily in my heart? Its cause was the plague that has affected every human since the fall of Adam. At our base, at our core, at the very heart of who we are since the fall of Man we have a sin nature. This sin nature is part of every man. Not one man, save Christ Jesus, has ever lived on the face of this earth that has not been infected with this horrible and deadly plague called sin. This sin nature is what houses our demanding spirit and our dangerous pride. This sin nature, this demanding spirit, and this pride is what prevents us from gracefully "Dancing with the Trinity."

I learned about my personal pride in a funny way many years ago. It was in a counseling session with an old backwoods farmer-type fellow when I first clearly recognized my pride for what it was.

This old farmer had been told I might be able to help him get through a significant loss in his life. I believed that I could help him understand and work through a normal grieving process. At the end of our first meeting I shook his hand and said I will see you Tuesday. The following Tuesday came and went without as much as a word from the farmer. His not showing for the next appointment surprised me a little. However, I thought that he probably didn't feel as though I had been much help and had just decided to not come back.

Several weeks passed, and on a Tuesday there stood the farmer at my office door. Slightly startled I said, "Well, hello, what brings you by my office today?" He said (in a very southern, country drawl), "Wayll hits Toosday and you'ns say-ed I could drop by." I was able to restrain my inclination to laugh and said, "Come in." That's when my lesson in pride began.

After asking him to sit I started trying to explain to him that when I had offered for him to come back on Tuesday I meant the following one, not any one of his choosing. I spoke of my busy schedule and my responsibilities over the various hospital departments and hundreds of hospital personnel. As a mental health professional and a hospital administrator my duties were important and many times the demands on me were immediate. As politely as I knew how, I asked him to please keep this in mind. The farmer replied, "Wah hell that haint nuttin. I've had me a job with hunderds of people neith me too!" "Really!" I said. "Yup," said the farmer. "I used to cut the grayss at the local cemeetary." There was a brief pause by the farmer, then a wink and some laughter (at me, not with me).

I had just been appropriately "had." This farmer put me in a place that I had needed to be placed a long time ago. The place was a realization of the fact that I was proud. I had long ago lost the idea that if I was important it was only because of God. Furthermore, my "importance" in a certain field or area didn't spill over to the fact that I was more important than anyone else. It might be true that I had some talent. It also might be true that I had received a level of gifting from God. However, what was most important is a fact that I had long ago forgotten. My gifting was from God and not of myself. What talent I might possess had been graciously given to me for the purpose of using in the service of others. Those "others" were precious souls that God loved dearly, and as His child I was to come to understand and view them as He did – absolutely precious. I was to use what God had granted to me for His glory to serve those in need.

I can't remember the farmer's name, but even as a nameless person he left an indelible impression on me that lasts to this day. Thank you, God, for Mr. Farmer.

Pride is the main tool in Satan's vast arsenal. Pride is the exact opposite of being "poor in spirit." The consequences of living pridefully are vast. A prideful person develops a critical spirit. A person filled with pride becomes judgmental. A prideful person can even become indifferent towards others. As the attitude of indifference develops, a person becomes more selfish. This selfishness runs contrary to what Jesus teaches about the blessedness of being meek. A person who is unwilling to become meek in spirit, to harness their will, and submit themselves to do the will of God experiences many serious consequences for that choice. A selfish person develops a stubborn and rebellious spirit.   This stubbornness and rebellion produces anxiety and anger. When you add those character qualities together you find that this type person tends to live life irresponsibly. Living in rebellion instead of obedience brings about death and destruction. All of this pain in life comes from one deciding to satisfy the desires of the flesh instead of being led by the Spirit of God. When our hearts become bent on meeting the needs of our fleshly desires the destruction takes root and flourishes.

In his letter to Galatia (Galatians), the Apostle Paul writes this: "Now the deeds of the flesh are evident, which are: immorality, impurity, sensuality, idolatry, sorcery, enmities, strife, jealousy, outburst of anger, disputes, dissensions, factions, envying, drunkenness, carousing, and things like these of which I forewarn you just as I have forewarned you that those who practice such things shall not inherit the kingdom of God," (Galatians 5:19-21). Satan uses these tools of pride and selfishness to divide and to destroy. Pride and selfishness are ultimately what prevents us from having and experiencing unity. Because pride always leads to selfishness, we fail in both our human relationships and in our relationship with God. It is pride that prevents a willingness to forgive. Forgiveness is necessary for restoration and reconciliation to occur.

Forgiveness: The World Can't Understand It, and Most Christians Don't Know What the Bible Teaches

Most Christians would tell you that forgiveness is a primary theme of their faith. That is a true statement. *However, I contend that many Christians do not understand what the Bible teaches about forgiveness and therefore live far beneath the Koinonia fellowship of unity that God intends with each other and with Him.* Many Christians remain trapped in a life of pride and selfishness because of their lack of the knowledge of what the Bible actually teaches about the giving and receiving of forgiveness.

I am under no allusion that every part or nuance of the topic concerning Biblical forgiveness will be answered in this chapter. My intent is purely to emphasize the absolute essentiality of studying and coming to a deeper level of understanding concerning this central theme of our faith called forgiveness. It is at this point that I must restate the necessity of doing the Bible studies at the end of each chapter. This is especially true about topics such as Biblical forgiveness. Because of the lack of understanding about what the Bible does teach concerning this subject, part of what you will read in this section could prove to be controversial. Please don't just read my thoughts and understanding on this subject and either agree or disagree with what I have written. It is so important that you view all of what is written in this book, and for that matter what anyone is teaching, through the eyeglasses of God's perfect and holy word. God's word is the only source of absolute truth!

If I do not understand the definition of a word, it would be almost impossible, or merely lucky for me to use that word appropriately in a conversation. So it is with Biblical forgiveness. If a person does not have a firm grasp on what the Scriptures teach about how we are to handle situations where we have been offended or perhaps when we have been the offender, how can one be expected to be able to effectively seek or offer forgiveness as God intends?

Church congregations are filled, perhaps dominated, by those who do not adequately understand God's requirements on forgiveness. Therefore, their ability to appropriately obey these directives is null and void.

It is a sad fact to me that the church does not adequately teach on the centrally important topic of forgiveness. I believe the failure to adequately teach on this topic is due to the false assumption that we, as the forgiven, understand the idea and principle behind Biblical forgiveness. This is just not true. *If we did understand the Biblical mandates surrounding the principle of forgiveness then the "Church" would be known both within itself and the unsaved world as a forgiving community in the proper Biblical sense of the word.* It is not.

I have read many books on the topic of forgiveness. Most of these books are not very good. Some of these books are outright embarrassments. I say that because most do not address forgiveness as a chosen action of obedience to God. Most books approach this subject as being some emotional response to a severing or falling out in our relationships. This is not what the Scriptures teach. Most of the material out there on the shelves has been written based on faulty beliefs or ideals from secular psychology or confused Christian psychologists. These poor attempts have bought the world's cheap substitute of apology built on sorry feelings. Feeling sorry can, at best, lead to the insufficient act of an apology. I truly hope I have piqued your interest with that last statement.

Apology is to Forgiveness as Oil is to Water

In the "For Deeper Insight" section of this chapter we will look at some of the scriptures surrounding Biblical forgiveness. It will become clear as you read those passages that God's word does call for forgiveness. As you come to understand forgiveness, you will also begin to recognize that the world settles when it allows for an apology. There is absolutely no mention of apologizing in the Bible. The idea of an apology is completely unscriptural.

The whole idea or concept of apologizing is interesting when one takes a serious look at the "word" history. An apology is a defense. An *apologia* was a defense made at a court trial in ancient Greece. Well, if one is offering a defense of some action, it seems rather ridiculous to assume that they are at the same time admitting a wrong and showing any degree of repentance. Through history the word has evolved to a softer usage and has come to mean, "I'm sorry." But to say, "I'm sorry," is not saying, "I have sinned." To say I am sorry does not say that I have sinned against God and I have sinned against you. The whole idea of apologizing either from the history of the word or from its present "softened" use is not an effort to come to a Godly sorrow for the wrong that has been committed. An apology does not place oneself in a humbling cry for forgiveness. The importance of understanding the difference between the world's apology and a genuine effort to come to and express Godly sorrow is central to being able to respond with Biblical forgiveness. The act of extending forgiveness to someone as God has forgiven us requires a confession of sin and seeking forgiveness, with Godly sorrow, for the wrong action. This is true whether someone is asking us for forgiveness or if we are the ones in need of

Biblical forgiveness. If the effort of expressing sorrow for a sin and seeking forgiveness for that wrong is present, then we are obligated to respond as God has towards you and I when we confessed a sin and sought His forgiveness. It is neither our responsibility nor our right to make a judgment of a person's heart. We can only respond to the outward action of the person seeking our forgiveness. At the same time extending Biblical forgiveness cannot be the response to the defense of an action or an individual who is unwilling to own the sin of their word or deed.

What Forgiveness Does and Is

Have you ever been asked a question that you feel you immediately know the answer to? How would you respond to a question like: **What is forgiveness?** What is the nature or essence of forgiveness? When all the false ideas and masquerades have been eliminated or boiled away, what is the irreducible element that makes forgiveness what it is truly meant to be according to God's Word? I believe that many of you will begin to realize that what you thought you knew about this subject is worth a second look!

For many years I have done seminars on a variety of topics such as marriage enrichment, spiritual retreat weekends, developing relationships, and teaching church leaders how to develop counseling ministries within the local church. In each of these seminar/retreats there is a point where I speak on the topic of Biblical forgiveness. I do this because of the centrality this topic holds to all that is Christian. Not only have I done this in specific group settings and to large congregations, but also in the counseling office with couples and individuals. It is vital to come to an accurate understanding about the concept and meaning behind Biblical forgiveness.

One thing that must be recognized about forgiveness is that it is "of God." God has created forgiveness. Forgiveness is something that He presents to you and I as a precious and holy gift. God is constantly, consistently, righteously, perfectly, and justly forgiving us. Both the Old and the New Testaments speak to the grace and power that are exhibited through God's gift of forgiveness.

Another important point to recognize about forgiveness is that God not only extends His forgiveness to us but He also gives very specific instructions as to how we are to forgive one another in love. "And whenever you stand praying, forgive, if you have anything against anyone; so that your Father also who is in heaven may forgive you your transgressions. But if you do not forgive, neither will your Father who is in heaven forgive your transgressions," (Mark 11:25-26). In Matthew's account, upon hearing the words of his Savior Christ Jesus (Matthew 18:35) it states, "So shall My heavenly Father also do to you if each of you does not forgive his brother from your heart." Also in Matthew from Jesus' Sermon on the Mount (Matthew 6:14-15) our Savior says, "For if you forgive men for their transgressions, your heavenly Father will also forgive you. But if you do not forgive men, then your Father will not forgive your transgressions. For these listed passages, and many, many more, you will see that the act of forgiveness is central to all that is in our faith and our relationships.

Forgiveness is not a feeling! God requires us to forgive our brothers and sisters whether we feel like it or not. Unlike modern discussions of forgiveness, there is nothing in the Bible about "feelings of forgiveness" or "having forgiving feelings" toward another. No, that is clearly the wrong path toward the understanding of this thing called forgiveness.

If you were to engage in a word study on forgiveness, and I hope you do, you will quickly find yourself reading Ephesians 4:32. This passage says, "...forgive one another just as in Christ God forgave you." Among other things you and I must first realize is that this forgiveness is to be modeled after God's forgiveness. So in order to find out what forgiveness is we must study God's forgiveness. It is in understanding God's forgiveness that we will be able to come to understand what our forgiveness should look and be like.

When Jehovah God forgives, He does not simply sit in the heavens and exude the warm-fuzzies. So forgiveness isn't a feeling. When God forgives He goes on record. He says so. He declares, "I will not remember your sins," (Isaiah 43:25). That statement alone should conjure up great excitement. Our spiritual selves should be stirred to the very depths of our soul in the understanding that God has decided to release us from the debt of our sin while actively electing to remember our sin no longer. When God forgives you and me, He lets us know that He will no longer hold our sins against us. If forgiveness were merely an emotional experience of God's, we would not know that we were forgiven. God's forgiveness is not a mere emotional experience; it is an act in which God declares that the matter of sin has been dealt with once and for all!

If God declares or goes on record concerning His forgiveness, what is it that He is declaring? What happens when God goes on record saying that our sins are forgiven? Well, the first aspect of action in the forgiveness is that God makes a promise. Forgiveness is not a feeling; forgiveness is a promise. Never forget that fact. It is one of the most stupendous facts of all time. When our God forgives us, He promises that He will not remember our sins against us anymore.

With that point in mind concerning God's forgiveness let me ask a second question: **Does human forgiveness exactly match God's forgiveness?** The quick and easy answer to this second question is, "No."

While we have been given the example of His forgiveness to follow as we forgive others there are indeed differences between the forgiveness that God can give and the forgiveness that we in our humanness are capable of extending. The most important difference is the fact that God is God. We are not. God is self-contained. By that I mean that God needs nothing outside of all that He is. Due to this fact, when we sin our sin does not somehow alter God, His nature, or personality. Our act of repentance or lack of the same does not in any way change God. God is the same: yesterday, today, and forever. This is not always the case when someone sins against us. This is especially true if the wrong against us results in devastation or has catastrophic results. Our emotions are altered and the act of forgiveness in these circumstances proves to be near impossible even if we are committed to obedience and sincere in our efforts to forgive.

If a person has repented of a wrong and has expressed a need for forgiveness from you with Godly sorrow, then you can forgive them. I say that you can forgive them, but actually Jesus in His teaching on this subject has said that under such a circumstance one would be obligated to forgive. When you forgive the offender you make them a promise to no longer hold bitterness and resentment towards them resulting from their wrong behavior. You will not hold the sin against them from that point forward. This promise that we make is an act of the will and can only be accomplished through a dying to self and allowing the Holy Spirit to direct our acts and to heal our hearts in these situations.

God is perfectly able to keep His promise to remember our sins no longer. This idea highlights what is yet another difference between the forgiveness that we give and God's perfect forgiveness. While we might determine to not focus on the sin of the forgiven our ability to remember no more is not there in and of ourselves. When we are able to come to that point in our lives it is a result of a healing that has come from the Holy Spirit acting as a salve to our souls.

There are times when "extending" forgiveness is not warranted but should be sought between believers. When one believer is wronged, they are not obligated to express or to extend forgiveness to someone who is not repentant. The unrepentant person hasn't reached and recognized Godly sorrow. In a situation such as this the believer that has been wronged *is* obligated to plant the appropriate seeds and water effectively in hopes that God brings this person to repentance. Remember, as the mature Christ-follower you must come to a spirit of forgiveness, fueled by grace and love towards the offender. This is a chosen act of obedience to follow the Biblical mandates regarding forgiveness. Whether or not you are given the opportunity to share or extend your forgiveness to the offender depends on their ability to receive it by being clothed in repentance and Godly sorrow. As a Christ follower you are always to forgive the person.

Your heart should be about the business of forgiveness regardless of a person's coming to Godly sorrow or repentance. As a believer, the offended person should prayerfully determine in their heart to have forgiveness present for their brother or sister in Christ. If the offender owns their sin they can participate in the joy of experiencing that forgiveness being extended to them. This is an interesting component of Biblical forgiveness. Having forgiveness present, ready, and available to extend is imperative. Remember forgiveness is not a feeling, but it is a choice that must be made in light of the forgiveness that we have received from God through Christ Jesus. Coming to a spirit of forgiveness is an act of obedience. The need to have forgiveness in our hearts is for our good. It is for our protection. It is for the good of all believers. This charge to forgive has been given to us by a jealous God that has already given us His best through His Son.

The gift of His Son to us is the gift of perfect love. Because of this perfect gift, the Christ follower cannot remain in bitterness and an unforgiving spirit towards others and expect to be able to approach the throne of God in spirit and in truth. It is impossible to remain in bitterness and an unforgiving spirit and expect to be able to Dance with the Trinity. However, not all wrongs will result in the experience of extended forgiveness. Extended Biblical forgiveness cannot be the response to the defense of an action or an individual who is unwilling to own the sin of their word or deed. This approach to extending forgiveness is modeled after God's forgiveness of our sins resulting in our salvation. This act of outward or extended forgiveness is unmistakably conditioned on repentance and Godly sorrow.

If another believer is not willing to own their sin then the mature believer must be willing to exhibit a bold love toward the offender. The mature believer should prayerfully move towards that person in an effort to bring them to a deeper understanding of their wrong. Maturity in Christ speaks to the hurt and devastation of the offender's actions with truth and in love. The mature believer should boldly love for the purpose of bringing another to appropriate sorrow and repentance for their sake and the cause of Christ. Even so, an impasse can exist between two believers when there is non-repentance or when forgiveness is not given to the repentant person showing Godly sorrow when it is appropriately asked for. As I will mention later in this chapter there may be the need for additional steps in situations like this to make what is wrong between two believers right before God.

Can an Unbeliever be Forgiven?

Based on the idea that our forgiveness is to follow God's example of His forgiveness towards us, one can make a reasonable inference about the unbeliever and forgiveness. The unbeliever cannot receive "extended" forgiveness from a believer. Again, as a child of God you must prayerfully work to have forgiveness in your heart and to be prepared to extend this forgiveness when appropriate. You must pray for that unbeliever to come to Christ. You must come to forgiveness of this person and ask that God will use your spirit of forgiveness in their lives to bring them to repentance and Godly sorrow. Yes, you must do this – forgive, even the unbeliever! That being true you must recognize both the need and immediate opportunity to share the Gospel with the unsaved. This opportunity could be the avenue that God uses to bring that person into the fullness of relationship with Him through Christ Jesus. Let me *briefly* explain.

The unbeliever has not accepted the precious gift of salvation from his loving God. The unbeliever has not recognized his need for forgiveness. Due to his sin nature, lack of Godly sorrow, and unrepentant heart he remains separated from God. They have not recognized their depravity and need for a Savior. If all of this is true, it is logical to then infer that they lack the ability to know and come to Godly sorrow for the wrong they have enacted against the believer. The increased need to pray for, to long for this person to repent is now obvious. The unsaved person desperately needs to come to a saving knowledge of Christ Jesus. What an open-door opportunity to witness when this occurs. The believer must take the opportunity to explain the difference between his willingness to accept an apology and his not being able to extend the Biblical forgiveness that he has already prepared in his heart for the unbeliever. It is not a rejection of that person to explain the necessary difference of apology and extended Biblical forgiveness. Actually it is just the opposite from rejection. It is a wonderful opportunity that should result in a loving pursuit of the unbeliever to come under God's grace, mercy, and authority.

As believers or Christ followers, <u>we must always have forgiveness in our hearts for *any* situation</u>. We must always be on the ready to give this holy and valuable gift. The only way to be able to do this is by practicing the art of living well in love (a topic addressed in a later chapter). It may be that we will never see repentance and/or Godly sorrow. It may be that the offender may even continue in their evil ways. Regardless it is necessary for our souls and for Christ's sake that we ask our God to help us forgive, to teach us how to forgive in accordance with the Scriptures. We must ask His Spirit to change our hearts so that we become not only willing but also able to forgive, even the unforgivable. When we do these things the very moment we recognize repentance and Godly sorrow, because we already have forgiveness in our hearts, this loving, healing gift is to be immediately extended to the offender. This is true in all situations. It is important to remember when we are faced with a person that is not repentant or a person that is not a Christ-follower we must still have forgiveness in our hearts. It is in this act of readied forgiveness that comes from living in love, that we have the ability to show them Jesus as we Dance with the Trinity. It is when we refuse to accept this difficult Biblical teaching about forgiveness that we ourselves remain in bitterness and resentment. When we pitch our tents in the lands of bitterness, when we set our camp on the foundation of resentment, we can't dance. We are left with the paralyzing effects of our rebellion and can only limp along in our pain.

It is this wonderful gift of forgiveness that allows us to respond graciously and positively when opportunity presents itself. When we have this opportunity we must speak of the important things of God with others so that they can come to know and have intimate relationship with God as well. The barrier to being able to Dance with the Trinity comes when we do not obediently trust God in our relationships. When we choose to glorify God in obedience, it is then that relationships can experience the unity and intimacy to which Christ Jesus calls us.

It is Important to Act Quickly

There is one more important point that must be made as it relates to Biblical forgiveness. Even intelligent and reasonable minds disagree. Even those with the most sincere motives and innocent thoughts find themselves in conflict. The most sincere Christian can be at odds with another believer at times. When this occurs there is a process that must be started immediately.

Jesus Christ gives us the instruction to "go to" whether we are the offender or the offended. In one situation the offender should "go to" and repent, asking forgiveness for their sin. In the other situation the offended should "go to" the other to rebuke and bring to repentance and then forgive. The first instruction is found in Matthew 5:23-26, and the second is in Luke 17:3-10. If reconciliation does not occur, next one must employ the process of church discipline outlined in Matthew 18:15 and verses following. I am briefly pointing out this process due to the extreme importance of making a bad situation right before God quickly.

In the cited scripture from Matthew 5:23-26 there are two phrases that stand out: "Go first" (v. 24) and "Quickly come to terms," (v. 25). Both of these phrases stress the urgency of reconciliation between believers. The idea of "first" being reconciled before continuing an act of worship is striking. Urgency is stressed. But also, God insists you must be on good terms with your brothers and sisters if you expect to remain on good terms with Him. The Scriptures are clear. Christ expresses the urgency. I am sure that you have heard the statement that "time heals all wounds." Regarding relationships this statement is just not true. When an offense is not addressed it festers; it does not heal. When points in a relationship have been broken and not dealt with effectively according to the Scriptures, our hearts become wounded and scarred. Instead of getting better and stronger our hearts become sicker with pride and selfishness and the atrophy of an unforgiving spirit sets in. Whether you are the offender or the offended, if there is a rift in a relationship between yourself and another (a spouse, a family member, a friend, or another person from the church) you are obligated to go! Furthermore, you must go quickly!

Too Much for Such a Small Space

The topic of Biblical forgiveness is far too important to be ignored in a book on relationship. At the same time, Biblical forgiveness is also far too important to pretend that it can be covered as a section of a chapter within a book on relationship. It is so important to understand the principles surrounding Biblical forgiveness. The Biblical teaching on this subject is central to all of our relationships. Because most do not know or understand what the Bible teaches they consistently live far beneath what God intends in relationship with Him and with one another. I have just scratched the surface on this topic. Biblical forgiveness is more than part of a chapter in a book. To go deeper would require the total focus of another book, perhaps volumes.

The subject needs to be adequately studied and therefore demands time in the Scriptures and some strong scholarly works to help us understand what the Biblical instructions are as it relates to forgiveness. Forgiveness, or the lack of forgiveness, is of primary importance in all of our relationships. Because of sinful pride the lack of forgiveness is the chief barrier to Christians being able to appropriately accept true repentance and move towards reconciliation and restoration. When understood and rightly applied, Biblical forgiveness is the avenue by which all relationships can experience healing and restoration leading to love and unity in the body of Christ as God intends.

I strongly encourage you to do a Biblical word study on this topic and recommend a tremendous work on this subject as a starting point for deeper study. Dr. Jay E. Adams has written what I consider to be the best apologetic (pun intended) on the subject of Biblical forgiveness. The title of his book is *From Forgiven to Forgiving.*

There are many ideas about forgiveness that people think are correct but in reality are seriously off base from the Biblical intent. When one looks deeply into the Scriptures they will discover that much of what the world has to offer are only imitations and cheap substitutes for what Jesus teaches about true forgiveness.

"A forgiving community is made up of forgiven people who have not forgotten that fact. Church congregations at their very best are composed of grateful people who DO remember the pit from which they were rescued (Isa. 51:1). They act neither shocked by sin in others nor superior to those in whom sin is found" (Adams, from *Forgiven to Forgiving*).

As you can easily see, this vast topic of Biblical forgiveness demands deep study and a strong commitment to learn what it is that God is trying to teach us about such an important part of all that it means to be a Christian. There are times when the act that has wronged us or the act that we have committed has created such devastation that coming to a spirit of forgiveness is just not immediately possible. This is true even when the offender is both sincere and expresses appropriate Godly sorrow. In these situations one must expect to go through and experience a severe grieving process. In a previous chapter sanctification was discussed and explained as a process that begins with salvation and continues through a life until one is glorified. In some situations working through grief and coming to forgiveness will take on the same character qualities as the process of sanctification. It too will require hard work, deep introspection, and intense efforts to submit to God's directives to come to a spirit of forgiveness.

The study section of this chapter will look at some scriptures that discuss pride, selfishness, and an unforgiving spirit. As you read through these passages, I suggest that you prayerfully approach God asking Him to reveal to you His lesson for your life as it relates to these negative character qualities. While it is true that as a believer you and I are no longer bound to our sin nature, we still struggle in all of these areas, and we must be willing to rely on the Holy Spirit to guide us towards attitudes of submissive obedience.

During this study ask the following questions: Do I have a prideful spirit at times? Do I ever behave in ways that could be defined as self-centered and selfish? Do I put my "rights" above others by being slow to forgive because I feel justified in my hurt and anger? Is my heart hard in any area of my life? These are extremely important questions and must be followed by one other question and request. The follow-up questions should be something like: What would it look like if I consciously chose to submit in obedience to God in these areas of pride, selfishness, and forgiveness? How would I be different? The follow-up request should be: Change my heart, oh God!

For Deeper Insight:

Pride

- A person that has a proud spirit is just the opposite of being "poor in spirit." Later in this book we will look at what Jesus promises the person with the attitude of being poor in spirit. But, for now, according to Luke 18:9-14, make a brief list of the differences between having an attitude of being poor in spirit and having a proud attitude.

- What do you think is wrong with being proud?

- In the Book of Revelation Jesus has a message for seven churches. The church at Laodicea was a proud church. How did Jesus point this out to them? What advice or counsel did our Lord give to them?

- Some of our Savior's harshest words were directed toward the Pharisees. Take a look at John 8:3-11 and then write down in your own words what Jesus Christ said to the Pharisees that lived in their pride.

- Look at the following passages in the Book of Proverbs. What do these verses say and teach about a spirit of pride?

- Proverbs 8:13; 11:2; 13:10; 14:3; 16:18; 29:23

- According to 1 John 2:15-17, what is the source of the pride of life?

- 1 Peter 5:5-10 and James 4:1-10 have some interesting steps that you might use to confront any pride that might be in your life. Take a look at these two passages and prayerfully ask God to help you rid yourself of this negative attitude.

Selfishness

- It is impossible for a person with a selfish spirit to surrender his rights (or ownership) to God. Therefore, it is also impossible for that same person to please God. When a person behaves selfishly, they are focused on satisfying the flesh. When that is their focus, their eyes cannot be on the Cross, and they are incapable of living a life worthy of the Gospel.

- Look at the following scriptures and write in your own words what each one says about a mind that is focused on self and the world instead of being focused on God: Proverbs 14:12; Romans 8:6-8; 12:1,2; Galatians 6:8; Philippians 2:5; 3:18,19; 4:8; Colossians 3:2, 5; James 4:4; 1 Timothy 5:6; 2 Timothy 2:4, 22; 3:2-7; 1 Peter 2:11; 1 John 2:15-17.

- Selfishness and self-centeredness, being focused on the flesh and the world instead of keeping your eyes fixed on God, is indeed a dangerous place to be. Ask God to help you keep your eyes on the Cross. Ask Him to fill you with His Spirit and to allow you to take the necessary steps to rid yourself of a selfish heart. In a spirit of humility ask God to change your heart. Ask God to help you have a heart that longs to follow Him only.

Unforgiving Spirit

- When we are in the midst of conflict most of our attention is usually on being heard and making others know that we are right. What would happen if one were to change that focus to Glorifying God in the midst of conflict and its resolution?

- Look at the following scriptures: Psalm 37:1-6; Mark 11:25; John 14:15; Romans 12:17-21; 1 Corinthians 10:31; Philippians 4:2-9; Colossians 3:1-4; James 3:17-18; 4:1-3; 1 Peter 2:12. What do these scriptures say about keeping our hope and our focus on God instead of on our own desires? What do they teach about depending on God's forgiveness, His wisdom, power, and love as we pursue a cure to a conflict in mercy and a forgiving spirit?

- One of the last feelings we usually have in a conflict is gentleness. However, we are obligated to "gently" restore relationships with our brothers and sisters in Christ Jesus. How do the following scriptures help us to understand the way we should behave in efforts towards restoring and reconciling relationships? Proverbs 19:11; Matthew 18:15-20; 1 Corinthians 6:1-8; Galatians 6:1; Ephesians 4:29; 2 Timothy 2:24-26; James 5:9.

- Remember the world's cheap substitute is an apology. Instead of accepting a premature compromise, or worse yet, allowing a relationship to wither because we do not "go to" our brother, we must *be reconciled*. What do the following scriptures teach about forgiving others as God, for Christ's sake, has forgiven us? How do they instruct us to seek a mutually beneficial solution to our differences and protect unity within the body of believers? Matthew 5:23-24; 6:12; 7:12; Luke 17:3-10; Ephesians 4:1-3, 32; Philippians 2:3-4.

- What is Biblical forgiveness?

- Does human forgiveness exactly match God's forgiveness? If not, what are the differences?

- Are we required to forgive even if the offender does not exhibit Godly sorrow or ask for forgiveness? Are we required to forgive someone that continues to exhibit animosity toward us? Does God ask us to forgive them? Why or why not?

- Is it necessary to "extend" forgiveness to find intimacy with God?

~ Seven ~

Dance Lessons
That Lead to Obedience

Starting at the beginning is usually a logical approach
in any situation. For us to become graceful dancers with the
Trinity it is absolutely necessary for us to come to our own "In
the beginning." Our beginning, our Dancing with the Trinity
requires a spirit of repentance, Godly sorrow for having once
lived continuously in our flesh. We must also have the humility
to face the lessons that God will take us through because of His
jealous love. It is absolutely necessary that we come to terms
with God's view of us. It is imperative that we understand our
utter depravity and our need of a Savior. It is also necessary
that we walk in the understanding of the Biblical revelation of
the nature of God. All of these points have been addressed in
early chapters of this book. Frankly, God has His part down
pat. When, and only when, we are willing to be submissive to
His guidance will we be able to participate in concert with the
plan He has for us to become graceful with the Trinity on the
dance floor.

A little more than thirty years ago I started praying
about starting a counseling ministry within a local church
where I attended and served in leadership. This was the
beginning phase of a lifelong direction that God has taken me
as I have worked consistently through my years in healthcare

and formal ministry. With a few of my friends that held similar interest in the helping professions, we settled on the name Solid Ground for this counseling program. We based the name and the program's focus on helping individuals, marriages, and families by counseling from the Scriptures. The name, Solid Ground, was taken from a passage found in Matthew 7:24. We paraphrased that passage in an effort to underscore its meaning toward finding help via the Scriptures for a person's life. The paraphrase reads: "...building one's life on Solid Ground." This particular section of scripture is part of Jesus' Sermon on the Mount and is a teaching parable comparing a person living a life outside of the Biblical instruction and one that meets that Biblical instruction with commitment and obedience. As a young and newly trained professional I was naturally excited about putting my studied trade into practice and hoped that God would use my efforts to impact lives for His Kingdom.

When someone begins a new career it is normal to want to be the best they can be. There is an excitement about "getting started" in the adult world, of being a positive contributor to society. The new teacher desires to be able to "reach" all of his students teaching them and helping them to grow. The new attorney wants to bring about justice and/or protection for all they represent. New to the church, the pastor hopes he is able to bring as many people to Christ as he possibly can. The list could go on and on. As a young counselor I was no different. I longed to help, to solve, and to "fix" as many problems as possible in my early days.

One day I was speaking with a middle-aged woman who was presenting her issue through many tears. There was a box of tissues in my counseling office, a tool of the trade. I innocently picked up the box of tissues and offered them to her. She said in a strong voice, "I saw the box on the table, and if I wanted one I would have gotten it!" Right then and there I knew that everything didn't need "fixing!" In fact, some things were better left un-fixed, if you will, to allow the process of emotions to run their necessary and effective course. It was actually my discomfort that prompted me to offer the tissues. This woman knew she needed to cry. She knew it was important for her to resist the natural tendency to escape from her deep emotions. She knew this was what was necessary in order to move toward healing. Staying with her pain would lead her to the path she needed to walk in order to allow God to teach His lesson and to heal. I needed her to stop hurting because of my personal discomfort and, for me, the faster this could be accomplished the better.

Sanctification
A Necessary Part of the Dancing Process

We do want to feel better and generally we want to feel better fast! However, sometimes the need to walk through the process is as important as the end result or goal. It's like that with learning to Dance with the Trinity. It is a process. The word of God verifies this process in many places but let me just share one: *"For I am confident of this very thing, that He who began a good work in you will perfect it until the day of Christ Jesus,"* (Philippians 1:6). God is continually at work within us. He is making us complete for His purpose in His time.

Our Christian growth is indeed a process. As a brand new Christian there are several things that take place at the beginning of our new life in Christ. The immediate things or events taking place are: conversion, regeneration, justification, and adoption. However, unlike conversion, where we repent of our sins and make a decision to trust in Christ for our eternal salvation; or, regeneration, where God imparts a new life to us; or, justification, where God gives us right legal standing before Him; or even adoption, where God graciously makes us a part of His family; *sanctification* is a "progressive" work that continues throughout our time here on earth. Conversion, regeneration, justification, and adoption all take place at the beginning of our Christian lives while sanctification begins with that first day in Christ Jesus and continues each day that we live on this earth. Sanctification is a work that requires cooperation between God and man. The process is comprised of both positive and negative learning, shaping experiences. At times the process can be difficult but refining. Sanctification is God's action in our lives. The refining work of God through His indwelling Holy Spirit brings us to an understanding of what it means to be an image bearer of our Risen Savior, Christ Jesus. Sanctification is God's process for growing us for our good and for His glory! Let me explain:

"The brother in humble circumstances ought to take pride in his high position," (James 1:9). Whenever God takes a saint to a lowly state it is designed to accomplish something that only the process can do. Job learned that *"He reveals the deep things of darkness and brings deep shadows into the light,"* (Job 12:22). Job's trials allowed him to learn things about God, himself, and his friends that we all need to know as well. He assumed things about God that he had to recant: *"Surely I spoke of things I did not understand, things too wonderful for me to know,"* (Job 42:3). God reveals things in the dark places of circumstances that will be used to reveal something He wants you and others to know. He has sent you ahead to learn these things so that you and others

will benefit from your unique experience. God views this place where you receive these truths as a high position. The world views it as a place to be despised.

The account of Joseph is another good example of what I am trying to explain. Joseph learned many things about God during his captivity that was used later as a ruler over a nation. *"He called down a famine on the land and destroyed all their supplies of food; and he sent a man before them - Joseph, sold as a slave. They bruised his feet with shackles, his neck was put in irons, till what he foretold came to pass, till the word of the Lord proved him true,"* (Psalm 105:16-19). Joseph was also led to this high position. It was in his adversity that he was prepared to be the most powerful man in the world as a thirty-year old.

Both God and man have distinct roles in the sanctification process. Sanctification makes us become more and more free from our sin nature and allows us to become more and more controlled by God's Holy Spirit. This process moves us to becoming more and more like Christ Jesus in our earthly lives.

If we are to Dance with the Trinity, we must understand our low times to be times of preparation. It is in these difficult times we are to submit in absolute and complete obedience. We must resist our human instinct to fix, repair, and move on. We must learn to patiently pitch our tents on the foundation of God's leadership. We must camp in His presence in faith. In taking this step we enter into the process of availing ourselves to being filled with and controlled by the Holy Spirit. It is imperative that we take every advantage of the opportunity. For you see it is here, during those difficult times, that God wants to take us deep into intimate relationship with Him. It is in the low times that God prepares our hearts to become His so that we can Dance.

Getting in Shape for the Dance

In high school I earned several varsity letters in a variety of different sports. Training, practicing, and staying disciplined to a lifestyle that reflected my goal to improve in the various sports was an intricate part of my life during those high school years. Because this is a part of who I am it is easy for me to relate to the words that Paul wrote in his first letter to the church at Corinth. *"Do you not know that those who run in a race all run, but only one receives the prize? Run in such a way that you may win. And everyone who competes in the games exercises self-control in all things. They then do it to receive a perishable wreath, but we an imperishable. Therefore I run in such a way, as not without aim; I box in such a way, as not beating the air; but I buffet my body and make it my slave, lest possibly, after I have preached to others, I myself should be disqualified,"* (1 Corinthians 9:24-27). In 1 Timothy Paul writes: *"Fight the good fight of faith; take hold of the eternal life to which you were called, and you made the good confession in the presence of many witnesses,"* (1 Timothy 6:12). It seems obvious that in our Dance we must practice, we must train, and we must condition our minds, our hearts, and our bodies to submissive obedience to God. Like any endeavor that is worth pursuing there will be times that the conditioning will hurt. Sometimes it will not be what we want to do and the act of obedience will require great sacrifice. This act of choosing to live under authority is sometimes very, very hard. Practice usually is hard. But, practice is necessary in our lives. It is necessary in our family, in our work, in our church, but most of all in our Dance with the Trinity.

Should We Wear Robes or Not?

It is so important for us to learn what it means to dig deeper into our Dance with the Trinity. It will be through practice that we grow in our relationship with God. It will look like the examples that we have been given by the Apostle Paul concerning "running the race" and "beating our bodies into submission." In our pride and selfishness we sometimes get confused about various practice styles. We think that worship and worship styles should be a certain way. We can even believe that one approach to praising and worshipping God is better than another. This idea is just not true.

Some churches have their focus on what I like to call "teaching your brains out" regarding the word of God. They spend weeks on one verse and sometimes even a couple of Sunday morning services on one word within a particular verse. This is fine. Actually, if I were to reveal a personal preference I would tell you that I love to sit under that style of teaching moving through the Bible verse by verse. However, I know that there are plenty of people who would prefer a topical sermon for a teaching style. There are some churches that literally jump out of the building in singing and dancing to our God. The music is loud and has a strong beat. Sometimes the music is a rock style. Other times the music is a Caribbean beat, black gospel, or reggae. Still other churches touch souls with their robe-clad choirs singing classical hymns accompanied by huge pipe organs. It is not a matter of whether to wear choir robes or not. All of these worship styles are fine. Once again I'm sure that like me, you the reader, could say that one of these examples is something you like better than the others. But, they are all both legitimate and fine worship styles.

Some people raise their hands in praise. Others fold their hands reverently as they pray in silence. The truth is, it doesn't matter. It is not a man or a woman thing, or a choir versus an ensemble production. It's not a black or a white thing. It is about worship and praise to our God.

Dancing with the Trinity is not about a "one time" prayer of salvation. Coming to an understanding of your need for a Savior is extremely important. To fall on your knees in prayer asking God for His forgiveness of your sins and to ask Jesus to be Lord of your life is a crucial part of the Christian life. Actually, without this step you cannot expect to have true relationship with God. But there is more! Dancing with the Trinity is not about a "dunking" under the water in baptism. However, this act of baptism is imperative. While on this earth our Savior, Jesus Christ, gave us two ordinances to follow. They are Communion and Baptism. To be baptized in obedience to His teaching is vital to our walk with God. Dancing with the Trinity is not about speaking in unknown tongues or exhibiting other supernatural gifts. Once again, I am sure that you probably have a preference or prevailing belief regarding this issue. I am convinced that our God is all about putting the "super" in our natural.

Dancing with the Trinity is about a passionate pursuit of God. We need to pray for forgiveness and submit to His Lordship. We need to follow this decision in baptism. We need to be filled with His Spirit and open to His leading of our lives supernaturally. Because of our differences we will find comfort in differing worship styles. But, whatever the style, we need to practice. That practice should drive us to deeper thoughts and deeper studies about our God. *The challenge is to praise with all of our hearts regardless of the style. Dancing with the Trinity is about having intimate relationship with God.* It is about allowing Him to have more of us in our worship of who He is. It truly is about our learning what His Word teaches us about our nature (the nature of man), His nature (the nature of God), and the reality of the relationship that we have with God through Christ our Lord. Our God is the First and the Last. It is all about Him.

Practice and Digging Deeper

A lot of people don't know that Michael Jordan was cut from his high school basketball team. I know that sounds strange but in an interview with his high school basketball coach, the coach is quoted as saying: "There were 12 boys in our high school that could play basketball better than Michael could."

That is a very interesting statement about a man who is arguably the greatest basketball player to ever play the sport. If the statement that his high school coach made was true then something surely changed from MJ's high school days to the days of North Carolina basketball and then on to the NBA's most valuable player status. The simple answer is a deep desire to improve, to get better. To improve and to get better requires practice.

A few years ago my son and son-in-law challenged me. It was not a direct challenge by them, but the challenge was there all the same. The two of them were in training for the Chicago Marathon. As they set out on that day's nine-mile run my daughter and I went along with them on our bicycles. It was a hot early fall day on the southwest coast of Florida. The run was hard. I was so thankful for my bicycle. When we got back to the house I felt the challenge from within. I went in the house and put on some gym shorts and a pair of running shoes. The shoes were several years old and had only served as my "knock-around" shoes so far. They had never been used to run. Confident, even though overweight and terribly out of shape, I was sure that I could run a mile. After all, I used to be a cross-country runner in my younger days.

I told the guys and my daughter what I was up to. There was a mile-long course through some streets in my neighborhood; heading out the door I said, "If I'm not back in 20 minutes, come look for me," (knowing *that being gone that long meant I was probably dead in a ditch on the side of the road and would need to be picked up and hauled away*).

To keep this story short I ran my mile in about 13 or 14 minutes and actually thought I would die several times during my trek. However, that day started a new period in my life. I became a runner! I changed my daily routine to include a run each morning. As time went by my runs became increasingly longer. I could feel my body changing and growing stronger and leaner, actually getting in shape. I even trained for and ran in the Disney ½ Marathon the following year.

I have continued to run each and every day. My one pair of unused running shoes is now a collection of four or five pair of training shoes and competition shoes. I have T-shirts from the various 5, 10, and 15K races that I have participated in over the last several years. There is an exercise apparatus in the garage for sit-ups, push-ups, chin-ups, dips, etc… Unlike before, now there is an environment of exercise and training around my home.

The equipment is necessary. But it's not the most important thing. There is another ingredient that is essential to the training process. Without this ingredient all the support, equipment, and apparel goes for naught. The environment is without meaning if I do not personally participate. Without personal sweat and determination the rest is only the wrapping. It is the inside, it is the effort, it is the investment, it is the ME in the process that brings life to the training and running.

So it is with God. We have to invest ourselves into His plan for us so that we can be conformed to His likeness. We have to invest ourselves in the process of being sanctified! The necessary ingredient is our "running the race as to receive the imperishable prize" and "beating our bodies into submission" for the cause of Christ. The process by which we become image bearers of the risen Christ is submissive obedience and living in love. Obedience and living in love leads to dancing. Dancing with the Trinity is an act of loving obedience to God. If submissive obedience and living in love is the path for learning to Dance with the Trinity, how are we to get onto that path?

I know, that I know, that I know!

My Father never spoke of Santa Claus. I don't know if it was that he just didn't want to perpetuate the lies associated with Santa or that he just had a more creative way of focusing on Christmas. Instead of Santa my Father would tell me about the "Old Gentleman." I can remember as a small child asking for a bicycle for Christmas. My Dad indicated that the Old Gentleman was very much aware of my deep desire for the bike and he (my Father – maybe he was the Old Gentleman as well?) was "pretty positive" that the Old Gentleman was going to be bringing me a bike. "WOW!" I was the kid who knew he was going to get that new Schwinn bike that he had been dreaming about for all his life. It was solid black and had the really cool chrome handlebars. There was a hi-lo "kick-back" gear to help you go really fast! This was the coolest bike ever! As you might well imagine, my steps were light, my spirit was excited. My confidence level was bold and strong! I knew, that I knew, that I knew.

The innocence and the excitement of a child is a beautiful and wonderful thing. It is in this same type of innocence and excitement that God wants us to pursue Him with. God wants us to desire to be known by Him, to cry out that He would "search and know my heart." In His divine jealousy He wants us to be consumed by Him. While it is true that we can and never will know God in His fullness, it is also true that He has chosen to reveal parts of Himself to us. God in His deep desire to have relationship with us has indeed given us a glimpse of His divine attributes. Because of this we know things that are absolutely true about God. We know of His love for us and His provisions for our life. Just knowing this about the Most High should create within us a deep desire to dance. However, our obstinate sin nature does not easily yield in obedience to His loving call. In our sin we wrongfully create mere ideas of God so that we can make our lives work. In our sin we don't practice and passionately pursue thinking rightly about God. We tend to be more interested in creature comforts and including God in those comforts than we are in pursuing Him with passion whether our lives are working according to our desires or not.

Generally when times in our life are good we spend less time thinking about God. We confidently move without Him as though we have everything under control. Why is it that we run towards Him complaining in those times when our only meals in life consist of a glass of stale water and the bread of adversity? Why are our steps not light and our spirits not excited even in the times we identify as bad? Is our God merely an indulgent "granddaddy" there to supply all the things on our wish list? Does God exist for the purpose of making our lives more manageable and to keep us from falling and scraping our knees? Surely He is more! How is it that our confidence level about God is not consistently bold, strong, and secure? When it comes to the Most High why are we not like the excited child at Christmas that knows, that they know, that they know? The answer to these questions falls squarely on deficient and faulty faith. In shallow faith we do not meditate on God; we do not meditate on Who He is and His glorious attributes.

In the next chapter I will discuss who we are as Christians; what it means to live in faith and love will be addressed. But first I want to briefly lay a foundation about how to appropriately focus our faith in God.

Faith Versus Manipulation

A short while ago I was made aware of an article or blog on a Facebook page that was written by a Christian missionary family that had gone through the devastating experience of losing their young child to the ravages of a fatal disease. The process of grieving and recovery will perhaps last a lifetime for these parents.

In this blog the parents reflect on the hundreds of emails they received from people trying to encourage them during this difficult time. They spoke of prayerful support that was given from around the world. They also shared the challenges they received from people to "have more faith." On the day they buried their young child they received an email stating,

"God has spoken to me and has revealed that your child is not going to die." The writer went on the say, "You just need to rebuke this illness in the name of Jesus and the child's life would be spared." The person writing this email was adamant that this phrase (rebuke in the name of Jesus) be utilized placing extreme emphasis on the grammatical style of the prayer that the parents must pray. What a difficult time in the lives of these dear parents. The process of losing their child has driven them deep into their faith. The path they have obediently chosen is impressive. Their pain and faith journey is expressed in some of the following thoughts.

If you are the parent of small children, or even grown children for that matter, the mere mention of losing your child to death is horrific. It is only those parents who have lost a child that can truly understand the deep pain and grief associated with such an event. We believe that children are not supposed to die. We think that somehow the death of a child is unfair, unplanned, and runs contrary to God's perfect and holy will. Generally we tend to believe that the death of a child is just wrong. When a young person dies or when the parents outlive their children we tend to question why. It is not uncommon to hear the grieving parent(s) and others ask God things like, "How can this be?" "Where were You?" "Why didn't you act on our behalf to save our child?" "We cried out 'In Your Name,' Lord! Why?" "You could have healed them, why did you ignore our prayers?" All these questions are understandable, but all of these questions are wrong.

Equally wrong ideas are those statements about faith surrounding events such as this. You know the ones that I speak of. They are the statements offered in support and encouragement that I'm sure are well intentioned, like, "You just need to have more faith… then you will experience a healing." "Why don't you have the faith to claim this victory in Christ right now?" "If you speak and rebuke this illness in the name of Jesus, God will heal your child!" "You know that if your faith is not great, God will not act!"

There is truth or elements of truth in each one of these statements. There is indeed power in the Holy and precious name of Jesus! Should we call upon His name? Absolutely! However, depending on the focus or object of one's faith, these statements can also be entirely wrong and outside of Biblical teaching.

That last statement about faith will find argument within the Christian community. I neither fear nor withdraw from opposing opinions. Outside of foundational tenants found in The Apostle's Creed it is okay for us to differ on some ideas about God. However, in our differing opinions we should always hold a spirit and attitude of love and unity with one another for the cause of Christ. That being said, I want to challenge you on a deeper level to what you have just read. If you are tempted to respond by saying something like: "You don't understand. Why or even how could you have such an idea about faith? God does heal! God is not only able to heal, He is faithful to heal." I want you to know this clearly, I do understand and accept that point of view about God. I have been that Elder/Pastor that has, in faith, prayed for a physical healing. I have anointed a person with oil and have laid my hands on the cancer-riddled body that has been given no medical chance of survival. The result has been a miracle of God through the power of His Holy Spirit. I have witnessed a cancer-filled body be completely cleansed of that dreaded disease. The healing came instantaneously and completely. God in His infinite power and wisdom, according to His perfect plan, chose to heal that person when all other avenues pointed to certain death. With equal faith in God and in His perfect power to heal, I have prayed for healing over the life of the young 18-year-old comatose patient as their body slowly shut down, and they eventually died. Again, God in His infinite power and wisdom, according to His perfect plan did not prevent death from coming to that young person that day. Does God heal? Absolutely He does! Sometimes He chooses to heal physically and in miraculous ways. Other times He does not.

To bring further clarity to this issue of appropriately focusing our faith, I would like to share an account of Jesus' earthly ministry found in the Book of Mark 2:1-12. It is the story of Jesus healing the paralytic:

Jesus Heals a Paralytic:

A few days later, when Jesus again entered Capernaum, the people heard that he had come home. So many gathered that there was no room left, not even outside the door, and he preached the word to them. Some men came, bringing to him a paralytic, carried by four of them. Since they could not get him to Jesus because of the crowd, they made an opening in the roof above Jesus and, after digging through it, lowered the mat the paralyzed man was lying on. When Jesus saw their faith, he said to the paralytic, "Son, your sins are forgiven."

Now some teachers of the law were sitting there, thinking to themselves, "Why does this fellow talk like that? He's blaspheming! Who can forgive sins but God alone?"

Immediately Jesus knew in his spirit that this was what they were thinking in their hearts, and he said to them, "Why are you thinking these things? <u>⁹Which is easier: to say to the paralytic, 'Your sins are forgiven,' or to say, 'Get up, take your mat and walk'?</u> But that you may know that the Son of Man has authority on earth to forgive sins..." He said to the paralytic, "I tell you, get up, take your mat and go home." He got up, took his mat and walked out in full view of them all. This amazed everyone and they praised God, saying, "We have never seen anything like this!"

Let's take a deeper look at the question that is found in verse nine (9) of this passage. "Which is easier: to say to the paralytic, 'Your sins are forgiven,' or to say, 'Get up, take your mat and walk?' "

At first glance it would seem that to forgive sins would be the easier act to proclaim. If Jesus simply said, "Son, your sins are forgiven," how, at that particular moment in time would one, could one possibly know if that statement were true or not? Where is the evidence? How could one go about proving such a statement to be true? Wouldn't it be necessary to understand fully all the activities of Heaven in order to have a faith that could accept such a radical claim?

Our Lord and our Savior did not stop there with that simple statement of forgiving sins. In order for us to be able to believe in His authority, he did a physical act that left little doubt in the minds and hearts of those who were there to observe. But, back to the question... "Which is easier?"

I submit that the act of physical healing was the much easier of the two acts. To heal a physical ailment or deformity and make new for a time within mankind's space and time is a finite act. To heal the soul of a person and to cleanse that soul from all sin for all eternity is the much greater act of the two. Furthermore, to place our faith on the only One that can heal our soul for all eternity requires a much greater faith than the faith to accept the temporary physical healing that is evidenced before us in the here and the now.

The outcome of a circumstance isn't about our conjuring up a certain measure or level of faith so that *we* bring about the desired result. Nor, does it depend on us "believing" enough that God wants a particular this or that. This line of thinking, or faith as some might contend, is backward. It is the thought equivalent to: when I understand then I will have faith in God; instead of, I have faith in God so that I might understand the things of God. If one were to take a critical look at the book of Job, especially Job 1:1-20, they would have difficulty explaining his circumstances by a lack of faith or a grammatical glitch in his prayer. Can one accurately blame the Apostle Paul for a lack of faith in the Risen Savior? If not, then why was the thorn not taken from him (2 Corinthians 12:7-10)? Many times it is in the outcome that we are able to learn more about God, through our faith, whether healing comes or not. It is not our faith in an outcome that somehow produces a healing. It is our purposeful faith in the Healer, Jehovah Rapha that places us in relationship with Him thus in line to receive His many blessings. Some of His blessings can be, and are, physical healing. The more important thing, the deeper faith, comes through intimacy in our relationship with our Most High God. The faith of the Scriptures is not an emotional approach to God's Throne centered around His ability to do or not to do certain physical acts on our behalf. The faith of the Christian Scriptures is accomplished as we submit our lives to His purpose for our life by placing all of our faith on this omniscient, immutable, self-sufficient, divine, and eternal God. The testimony of faith is a simple fact that in its exercise is herculean. Faith is the trust and belief that regardless of how things appear in this "Glorious Ruin" (the fallen world), all of God's acts are fully His and are wrought in infinite and perfect wisdom. Faith is to be placed on Who God *Is*. Our faith is to be placed in Him and Him alone with no conditional regard to life's outcomes.

It is imperative that we take every advantage of the opportunity to pitch our tents of faith at the feet of God. By choice we must live in His presence. Otherwise we will live in weakness. When we live in weakness it is because we have allowed Satan, the master of deception, to pull a fast one on us. The *fast one* that Satan uses is to convince us to settle. When we become *happy* in our knowledge about God and view our knowledge as acceptable and sufficient - we settle. Because we can use some spiritual sounding words (God Talk) in conversation and can recall some of the Scriptures, we have the appearance of seasoned dancers. When we view this as enough - we settle. Satan loves our willingness to settle in our knowledge. If that is where we choose to reside then we don't dance. When we decide to settle it is because we have listened to the only argument that Satan has. Satan's weapon is to attack our faith by creating doubt. When doubt takes hold we then settle. To settle is proof that we haven't moved to the point in our lives where all that matters is that we *know God and are known by Him in intimate relationship*. When we settle we destroy our ability to step onto the dance floor. In chapter two I pointed out that in that truest of all loves you are able to find completeness. So it should be with God. When your completeness is found in God and God is the object of your faith you dance.

If we are going to dance, then we must position ourselves appropriately in relationship with God by living each of our days by faith in submissive obedience.   This faithful living can only be accomplished by living in love through the power of His Holy Spirit as we prayerfully move through the process of sanctification with God. We can only position ourselves rightly through practice. Our practice is digging deeper into His word. We practice when we worship and praise His holy name.   It is by knowing His word, by placing it in our hearts, and by living in faithful obedience that we are then able to begin to think rightly about God. I can imagine no greater exercise, no greater discipline than to commit to thinking rightly about God. For us to abandon our immature, wishful thinking about God is necessary. Thinking rightly about God is not just important it is altogether fitting and proper to focus appropriately on the very nature of the Most High God!

As we begin to consider what it means to rightly think about God, we must first come to terms that through the intellect of man God can never be known. Our understanding of God and any image that we may develop will come necessarily through the use of that which is not God. That is, we must draw from the things that we know about in order to have thoughts about that which we do not know.   God is truly known by no man. God is self-contained and incomprehensible in His fullness. The mere desire to know God comes from our being created in His likeness. Our ability to even think loftier thoughts about our Creator comes through His Spirit adding illumination to these thoughts. One needs to just think back to the times before they became a Christ-follower to understand the difference between walking in spiritual blindness and moving through life with God's new spiritual eyeglasses. We can never take for granted our ability to think about God. Our praise and thankfulness should be ever present towards this God that not only reveals to us His divine attributes but also allows us to contemplate all that He is. Deep does cry out to deep. Man longs to know, to love, and to experience His Creator. Our soul senses its roots and naturally longs to return to its source. The Bible is clear concerning the path that man must follow in order to think rightly about God. The only direction that will lead us to right thinking and right relationship is through His only begotten Son, Christ Jesus. It is through knowing Christ that we can begin to gain a glimpse of this God that came to us by way of incarnation. Through an act of atonement He reconciled us to Himself filling us with His Spirit. By faith and love we respond to Him, the One who has sought us and brought us unto His own. We must move from mere ideas or wishful thinking about God to the deeper thoughts of contemplating His divine attributes. We must press ourselves to begin to think lofty thoughts about our God. It is true that we will always be limited to think of God in human terms, but even now we can think rightly about God by abandoning our ideas and ideals about Him and just simply recognize that He is incomprehensible and above our understanding. We begin at the point where we acknowledge that God is Greater and that He is Holy. You and I have no greater calling than to focus rightly on His nature. It is in being rightly focused that we enter into intimacy with God. It is this focus that leads us to the Dance.

It is Time to Become Carnivores

The Apostle Paul called out the Corinthian Christians because he was unable to feed them the solid food of the Gospel. He commanded them to grow up! In Paul's estimation they had long ago decided to be "professionally weak" in the faith. Truthfully there was no excuse for them to not have the ability to digest the deeper things of God except for their unwillingness to act and be more mature in relationship with God.

When the "World" defines happiness, it usually identifies this in terms of having material wealth, controlling power or notoriety, and fame. How much material wealth would a person need to be happy? How much power or fame is necessary for happiness to be realized? I've known several people that had great material wealth. The richest person that I have personally known was worth about 200 million dollars at the time of their death. Their death came at the hands of a purposeful, self-inflicted gunshot wound. By anyone's measure this individual was wealthy. However, it was not happiness that led to their death, it was grief and despair. I've known others with powerful positions that lived in fear of losing their power and influence. The fear that they live in is not of God. The decisions they make in fear are at best reactive in nature and fall far short of decisions made with Godly wisdom. I've known famous individuals that lost all hope for peace because of their notoriety. Their lives were lived under the critical microscope of a public that couldn't wait to see them suffer and fail. Those that pursue material wealth, power, and fame do so at a tremendous cost. The cost is rejecting a life that is lived under and controlled by the Holy Spirit of God. By electing to serve the masters of wealth, power, and fame they lose the fruit of being led by the Spirit.

God's wisdom defines happiness in a completely different way from the world. God speaks of a happiness that can bring one the ability to live above the circumstances of life and have the ability to live a life free from any fear of what the future might hold. Jesus in His Sermon on the Mount presents this path to happiness clearly.

This Jesus is the One through whom all things were created. It is through His will that all things continue to exist as they are. It is this same Jesus that gave all so that we might be with Him and the Father for eternity. *"For we do not have a high priest who cannot sympathize with our weaknesses, but One who has been tempted in all things as we are, yet without sin. Let us therefore draw near with confidence to the throne of grace, that we may receive mercy and may find grace to help in time of need,"* (Hebrews 4:15-16). It is Jesus that points the way, by becoming like us in all our suffering, temptation, and disappointments, so that we can become like Him. The more we look like Jesus through the sanctification process, the more we become the true man or true woman that God has designed us to be. The more we live by His directive, losing our life for His sake, we obediently become who we truly were created to be. Becoming like Him means realizing a deep, deep sense of spiritual happiness that has absolute victory over what the world attempts to use to keep us in fear and doubt.

For Deeper Insight:

Running the race and fighting the good fight are our part of the sanctification process. Learning to live in obedience does require a deep commitment on our part to allow the Holy Spirit of God to work His way in our lives. It amounts to our desire to have "our cup" filled to its capacity with God and with God alone. It is only when this happens that we can begin to deal honestly with important questions for living successfully under His authority. Ask yourself these questions and prayerfully meditate on their answers:

- Do I truly desire that God would work in my life each and every day?

- When life throws me its inevitable curve balls do I respond to these difficult situations in faith and trust that God has even my suffering under His control?

- When I pray do I believe that God is hearing me? Do I believe that He answers the prayers that I offer?

- Jesus taught me to ask that God's will be done here on earth (in my life) just as it is in heaven. Do I truly long for this?

- Take a look at Philippians 2:5-11. How did Jesus model a life that is lived in obedience?

- 2 Corinthians 10:5-7 and Philippians 4:4-9 show how our thought life can be brought into obedience. Write down your thoughts about these two passages.

- What does 1 John 5:1-3 indicate proves our love for God?

- 1 Samuel 15 gives some good lessons about obedience. What can you learn from this passage? Saul of Tarsus, in Acts 9 also offers lessons on obedience. Write down what you learn in this passage.

- There are four indicators of an obedient Christian listed in Acts 2:42. What are they? List them.

- Now, meditate on the FOR DEEPER INSIGHT study in obedience that you have just completed. Write down two, perhaps three examples that are concrete evidence that you are growing in your obedience to God.

~ Eight ~

The Dance

In 1962 the editors of *American Heritage* magazine asked the then sitting President of the United States, John F. Kennedy, to write an article for their publication. The article was to be his assessment as to why knowing history is important for the American citizen. Some poignant quotes from this excellent article are as follows:

- "There is little that is more important for an American citizen to know than the history and traditions of his country."

- "Knowledge of our history is, first of all, a pleasure for its own sake."

- "A country's history is a statement of the values and hopes which, having forged what has gone before, will now forecast what is to come."

These are all powerful quotes from an extremely interesting and well-written article by this country's 35th President. However, my favorite point made by Mr. Kennedy regarding the importance of knowing history is: "A knowledge of history is, above all, a means of responsibility – of responsibility to the past and of responsibility to the future..."

So it is with the Christian. As Christians we should know our history. This is why God has been so careful to preserve

His word for all the generations. When you begin to study the word of our Holy God it becomes immediately apparent that the history of man is completed in faith according to God's plan.

So what is faith? *"Now faith is the assurance of things hoped for, the conviction of things not seen,"* (Hebrews 11:1). That quote is from the most familiar chapter in the book of Hebrews. The eleventh chapter of Hebrews is one of the most familiar and popular chapters of the entire Bible. As Christians it is our history. This chapter has been referred to as "The Faith Hall of Fame." The chapter is not just about faith, but speaks to the deeper point of faith in action. It is about faith at work, faith that stands strong in the face of battle, faith that is bold when confronted, faith that withstands pressure, faith that lives free in the face of persecution. While the author is, like all of Scripture, the Holy Spirit of God, the human tool used to pen this book and chapter is unknown. Even so, the picture that is painted is a masterpiece that has left the church through the centuries breathless, thrilled, and inspired. This is our history. We are a people of faith. This faith is our dance with God.

At this point you should have a clearer understanding of what it means to be created in the image of God. Part of what that means is that you and I are relational. It should also be much clearer to you that our dance partner, God, is both powerful and wonderful. We must be on our toes if we have any hope of keeping up with His leading in the dance. God is not a "thing," a power, or some type of influence. God thinks, that is to say He is rational. God is emotional, God is volitional, and God is relational. God is more than just "the man upstairs" or some kind of "superman." Jehovah is the true God. He is the living God. He is the eternal King.

The previous chapters have discussed some of the main barriers to becoming graceful in a dance with our holy, living, and loving God. Also, the earlier chapters have presented some ideas on how to practice your relational and spiritual dance moves. It is now time to discuss the specifics of the Dance with the Trinity. By that I mean, what is the basic criteria that we must avail ourselves to if we are to step onto the dance floor gracefully with the Trinity in relationship?

Be Like Christ

If therefore there is any encouragement in Christ, if there is any consolation of love, if there is any fellowship of the Spirit, if any affection and compassion, make my joy complete by being of the same mind, maintaining the same love, united in spirit, intent on one purpose. Do nothing from selfishness or empty conceit, but with humility of mind let each of you regard one another as more important than himself; do not merely look out for your own personal interests, but also for the interests of others. Have this attitude in yourselves which was also in Christ Jesus... (Philippians 2: 1-5). If you read further in that passage you will discover what Christ truly was like. You will see His attitude and His commitment to His purpose to "do the will of the Father." It is obvious that Jesus Christ was a servant.

If you recall, in the first chapter there was a listing of the "One Anothers" found in the Scriptures. God's purpose in Christ is to create a community, bound together in a common life that is defined or characterized by a bond of love through Christ Jesus. In this community called the church we should "fan into flame" the deep desire for all to express mutual encouragement towards one another to grow in their relationship and become graceful in their Dance with the Trinity. Philippians 2:1-5 directs clearly towards this end for every believer. The book of Philippians has been referred to as a book of "joy." In this particular passage of Philippians Paul is saying: "make my joy complete!" In other words, do more! Act in such a way towards one another that the joy that Paul speaks of can be even greater. Have an attitude and act in such a way that this joy could be even fuller as the unity of God's church becomes greater and greater.

A Servant's Spirit

Taking on the spirit of a servant is one way to participate in the dance. This servant's spirit is being like Christ. A person with a servant's spirit is someone that is dedicated to ministering to others both by their words and in their deeds. This spirit is exemplified in a person's life by acts that are certainly uncommon, if not altogether foreign, to the world's way of doing things. A servant of God is motivated by love and has as their goal unity in the body. They accomplish this by serving those placed in their lives by God. Their service is marked by actions that are sacrificial, deliberate, joyful, and voluntary. A person that has a servant's spirit will pour their life into the life of another for the benefit of that other person. They will pour their life into the life of the other person voluntarily, joyfully, deliberately, and sacrificially. Becoming like Christ will involve the development of a heart that desires to serve and then acts on that desire. Mark 10:45 states, "For even the Son of Man did not come to be served, but to serve, and to give His life a ransom for many."

One of the main points that Jesus expressed as He walked on this earth was that He had come "to do the Will of the Father." This act of doing the Father's Will was accomplished voluntarily. You see Jesus could always have opted out. Doing the Father's Will was done in a spirit of joy. Jesus taught and lived a ferocious love. Jesus' mission was purposeful and thereby deliberate. In the perfect attitude of a servant our Savior's sacrifice has no equal. It was a sacrificial act that was "once for All." No other act in the history of humanity can compare to the voluntary, joyful, deliberate, and sacrificial acts of Jesus. The life of our Savior sets the standard for what it means to be a servant. Being like Jesus commands a servant's spirit. A person with a servant's spirit is an image bearer of their risen Savior. As you and I learn to function with this attitude of servant-hood we will dance.

Living in Love

It was late fall in 1974. I was chilled to my bones from an Appalachian rain that had been steadily falling most of the day. Because of the rain I had not covered as many miles as planned that day - generally any where from twelve to fifteen miles a day; on a good day perhaps even twenty. This day I had only walked about five. It was slow going because of the rain and the terrain of upper east Tennessee and western North Carolina. There were endless "switch-backs" leading up one ridge then down another. The temperature was just above freezing so the rain was bitterly cold. Although it was cold, I had still managed to work up a pretty good sweat. At the top of one of the many ridges I stopped for a much-needed rest. To my amazement and joy several apple trees were about 250 feet from the trail. I dropped my backpack and headed for the apples. Jesse, my 105 pound golden retriever, was hot on my heels. When we got to the first grouping of apple trees, it couldn't have been more perfect. The fruit was large, ripe, and just begging to be picked. I gathered about eight or so apples and got one for Jesse as well. When we got back to the trail I saw a large rock overhang that I quickly decided would serve as our shelter for the night. Sitting under that large rock I started looking at those apple trees. They represented a sweet moment in what was otherwise a fairly miserable day on "The Trail" (Appalachian Trail). Staring at the apple trees, I began to notice something that struck me as very interesting. The trees were standing in this cold, late-fall rain effortlessly. They were filled to the utmost with splendid fruit. However, there was not even a hint of stress, work, or effort on the part of the tree. This was only possible because as the seed or seedling hit the ground years ago the work that was required of it was to dig deep and develop a root system. It would be through this root system that all the moisture and nutrients from the soil would be brought to the tree for growth and prosperity. This was the seed's part of what God had intended. In fulfilling its part the seed responded in obedience to God's perfect plan in Creation.

It is that work, developing a root system, that lies before each one of us in the Kingdom of God. *"But, his delight is in the law of the Lord. And in His law he meditates day and night. And he will be like a tree firmly planted by streams of water, which yields its fruit in its season, and its leaf does not wither; and in whatever he does, he prospers,"* (Psalm 1:2-3). Our roots must become firmly planted in the Word of God. We must dig deep to understand His directives and then lovingly submit to the direction He gives. This is what it means to "fall in love" with God and begin to dance in intimate fellowship with the Trinity.

"The fruit of the Spirit is love." Only as we live in love can we fulfill the will of God in our lives and dance gracefully with the Trinity. The believer must become love-inspired, love-mastered, and love-driven. Yes, the fruit of the Spirit is love, and this fruit, this love is manifested in joy, peace, patience, kindness, goodness, faithfulness, gentleness, and self-control. Joy is love's strength; Peace is love's security; Patience is love's endurance; Kindness is love's conduct; Goodness is love's character; Faithfulness is love's confidence; Gentleness is love's humility; Self-control is love's victory. No wonder the Scriptures proclaim, "Against such thing there is no law." A person that is led by the Spirit of God needs no law to direct them to live a righteous life. A person that is led by the Spirit of God has come to terms with God and has placed their life under His authority and control. In doing so they have peace with God and enter the Dance.

Bus

Many years ago I met Bus Wiseman. Bus was an evangelist/preacher who exhibited tremendous zeal for presenting the Gospel in a fresh and exciting way. His personal style was much like the Apostle Paul, but his heart looked like Jesus. He wrote a book of various Bible studies that I purchased and used for a couple of years. In my opinion the book is as powerful as Bus Wiseman's preaching. The contents of his book forces a person to get into the word of God and look at what the application of God's truth would bring into a life. In a physical move from one job to another, I misplaced this important book. After exhausting every possible alternative of where the book might be, I resigned myself to the fact that the book was lost. No problem, right? I'll just go to the local bookstore and order another copy (this was before the days of Amazon and online publishing). After many, many attempts trying to locate the book, a vender informed me that this particular book was no longer in print. - what to do? I loved this book and wanted to have a copy on my shelf to refer to and to teach from. After some thought and prayer I decided to give Mr. Wiseman a call.

Surely the author would have a few copies of this out of print book in storage somewhere, and I could purchase one from him. Bus told me he would send me a copy of the book, and I thanked him and hung up the phone. A few weeks later the book arrived.

In the front of this book Bus had written a loving note to his Mother. The inscription revealed the special relationship he had with this woman who brought him into this life. Sending me this book was an obvious mistake! I immediately called Bus and told him how he had mistakenly sent me the book that he had presented to his Mother as a loving gift several years ago. Bus said, "Rye, I sent that book to you on purpose. My Mother has passed on to be with Jesus. When I looked for another copy of my book the only ones I had were printed in Spanish. You convinced me that this book was important to you, and I sent you the only one that I had." Bus refused to allow me to return this book to him. Bus Wiseman is a man who has learned to live in love with a servant's spirit. Bus gave out of my need not his own. In doing so his life looked like Jesus in the things he did. I treasure the book to this very day.

Serving, Dancing, and Living in Love

Living in love can take many forms. There are several things that have become extremely important to me as I grow in my effort to live in love. Most are simple, but they are things that I treasure all the same. Many have risen to the top of my priority list in such a way that I try to do them most every year. I read A.W. Tozer's book: *The Knowledge of the Holy* every year. Each year on Martin Luther King, Jr. Day, I watch his "I have a Dream" speech/sermon, usually inviting people to watch this important message with me when the opportunity presents itself. We gather for the purpose of understanding the content of this message and how our lives stack up to Dr. King's charge and dream. In a somewhat silly way, I make Goundhog's Day a special event that is celebrated with cake and a huge family party.

Although these "important" things are radically different from one another they all speak to various elements in my personality and the unique way I Dance with the Trinity. These are small but significant things that have impact for me. They all serve me in my quest to develop and improve my relationship with God and with others. I engage in many different things that qualify as my effort to Dance with the Trinity. Some of these are more mundane, less systematic than others, but all equally important for me. Each day I focus on God's presence in my life. God and I have conversation (mostly He talks, I listen). I also focus on fulfilling the mandates of my calling as a husband and father. God has given me specific directives in these roles. I know that in my obedience to these directives He is given both glory and honor. There is another act that has significance for me. I study and usually teach a 9 to 12 week lesson on the Beatitudes each year. The lesson that I teach is from Bus Wiseman's book, *Discipling for Jesus*. I do this because of the importance of the content of the message that Jesus is trying to convey. It is in His Sermon on the Mount that we can see clearly how His kingdom is indeed upside-down from the world in which we live. As a person grows in their spirituality, as they mature in their faith, as they become more graceful on the dance floor, they recognize how attitudes necessarily change.

Changes in Attitude - The Beatitudes

The last paragraph has a statement that bears repeating: "As a person grows in their spirituality, as they mature in their faith, as they become more graceful on the dance floor, they recognize how attitudes necessarily change." In our old and sinful nature we have the attitude that we can do things on our own. We spend intense energy trying to prove that we are capable without any outside assistance. As we mature in our faith this maturity drives us away from ourselves and to the Cross of Jesus. As we come to understand our sin nature outside of Christ Jesus, we start the process of growth spiritually. Once again, this growth drives us away from ourselves and to the cross. In our spiritual growth we begin to move more gracefully in our relationship with God. This too, drives us away from ourselves and to the Cross of Jesus. As we are driven towards Christ, it is interesting how it is Christ that begins to lead us in the Dance.

As we begin to move towards Christ in intimate relationship, this will naturally draw us to His teaching. It was Jesus in His Sermon on the Mount that laid out for us the necessary attitudes to enter into the most intimate of relationships with Him and to find His blessings in our lives. We must first come to a few understandings about our lives *in* Christ before we can Dance with the Trinity.

Picture the setting of the day that has been recorded as the Sermon on the Mount. The crowds were large enough that it was necessary for Jesus to go and teach from the side of the mountain or at least a rather large hill. He did this so that He could be seen and heard by all who were present. You might even, with some imagination, see that Matthew could have viewed Jesus as a second Moses giving God's new law to the people. As Matthew watched the Messiah speak from the mountain it is possible that he envisioned Moses speaking from the mountain to the people of Israel delivering God's direction on how they should live for Him.

From Jesus' elevated position on the side of a hill, probably near the Sea of Galilee, He started telling His listeners how to experience joy and be in intimate relationship with Him. Jesus gives eight attitudes in the sermon that if lived will lead a person to happiness or being blessed. Each and every one of these attitudes is significantly important. However, I am briefly going to review only the first four. I am doing this because I sincerely believe that there is a progressive nature in how our Savior taught these attitudes. Furthermore, I believe that as we grow and begin to exhibit these first four attitudes daily in our lives through the power of the Holy Spirit, the remaining four attitudes will be as an out-pouring of the presence of the first four attitudes or beatitudes as they are named.

God's Upside-Down Kingdom

Poor in Spirit (Matthew 5:3) – Jesus says that the result of having an attitude of being poor in spirit is that you will have the Kingdom of Heaven. That is, that the Kingdom of Heaven will be yours if you live in the attitude of spiritual poverty. People that understand their spiritual poverty are those that realize that they themselves lack any power to do what God wants them to do. The spiritually poor person has put all his trust in God's ability to supply his spiritual needs. Because of this God-centered focus, a spiritually poor person may also be materially poor as well. This is not necessarily true, but it would also not be uncommon. The spiritually poor person has no room to place an emphasis on worldly possessions. Their entire focus is on God, and they choose to be ruled by God rather than being ruled by the pursuit of material goods. Their personal cup is filled with the things of God. When one comes to the realization that his primary need is for God, it is then that he has the Kingdom of Heaven.

Those that mourn (Matthew 5:4) – What a promise we have from Jesus concerning those of us that mourn! The promise is that we will be ultimately comforted. This promise of comfort goes beyond a value that can be described. It can only happen in His holy presence. When this happens we experience complete peace with God. We can experience aspects of this in the here and now, but ultimate peace with God will come at our glorification. Those that mourn, that feel deep sorrow and remorse for their own sins and failures, and for the evil that is ever present in this world that creates so much suffering, will one day know complete comfort from God. While we walk on the earth we are able to have this peace with God at levels that belie the circumstances we are experiencing. The comfort that God extends easily confounds the world because the world knows nothing of Godly sorrow.

The meek (Matthew 5:5) - How is it that our Savior promises the inheritance of the earth to those who are meek? Many people equate meek with being weak or being a coward. However, when Jesus spoke of being meek He had something quite different in mind. The meek person is the individual that trusts God. They trust God instead of themselves. The meek person is the individual who has literally moved to harness his will to do the will of God. The example of harnessing our wills to do the will of God was lived out perfectly by Jesus.

"...who, although He existed in the form of God, did not regard equality with God a thing to be grasped," (Philippians 2:6). A meek person understands his own limitations and puts his ultimate dependence on God. Psalm 37:11 states: "the meek shall possess the land." God gave a Promised Land to His people in the Old Testament. In Christ, as we grow in our dependence on God rather than ourselves, we will inherit a "new land of promise." Our day of our promise is coming!

"Those who hunger and thirst for righteousness" (Matthew 5:6) – I don't know about you, but I have never truly been hungry or thirsty. By design I have gone without food for 17 days. During that time I never experienced the deep, deep hunger pangs of starvation. My stomach did not bloat, and I was far from emaciated. When I imagine being thirsty, I think of the person who has been in the desert for days without water. His lips are cracked and dried. They are bleeding and sore from the lack of moisture. Even if water were available, at this point the most that could be done would be to gently wipe his lips with drops of water to not throw the body into a rejection type of shock. These examples are what it means to be truly hungry and thirsty. Physically most of us have never been there. Have you and I been there spiritually? Jesus said that those who do hunger and thirst for righteousness will be satisfied. Are we? To become satisfied in Jesus requires that we want, more than anything else, to see the world's evil (this would include what is wrong in our own lives) overcome by God's righteousness. Our commitment must be to do what is right in loving, submissive obedience. We must be able to truthfully pray to God asking that His will would be done in our life just as His will is being done in heaven. Our wills must want this righteousness as much as a starving person wants food and as much as a person dying of thirst would want water. With that attitude present, Jesus has promised that God's righteousness will ultimately prevail and that our desire for it will be fully and completely satisfied.

As I have said earlier, the presence and growth in the attitudes of spiritual poverty, mourning over the sin, the evil that is of this world, harnessing our wills in meekness to do God's will, and hungering and thirsting after righteousness will result in the remaining four attitudes developing within our lives. As we learn to live by the Spirit of God we will exhibit mercy. The purity in our hearts will increase as we mature. Our action will be that of a peacemaker. And, with this will come persecution because of the righteousness in our lives. As our attitudes begin to reflect the evidence of being "in Christ" we dance. We gracefully Dance with the Trinity.

The Church, Its Purpose

Satan uses our failed relationships here on this earth to convince us that any attempt to be intimate with God cannot be trusted. Satan does this by the simple method of creating doubt. In creating doubt Satan then moves to challenge our faith. Don't forget our history. We are people of faith. We must learn how to always live in this faith as we approach the throne of God. Let me remind you that your battle, our battle in this life is against principalities of darkness in the spirit world. It is not against flesh and blood. Jesus only mentions The Church two times in His teachings. The first mention is found in Matthew 16:18 where he claims the power of the Church against the assault Satan and his army bring against it ("…and upon this rock I will build my *Church*; and the gates of Hades shall not overpower it"). Secondly, in Matthew 18 verses 15 and following, Jesus gives a process of love to help someone escape the snares of chosen sin.

First we are to "go to" one another one-on-one. If this fails, then take others to confirm the truth. Again if at this point in the process there is still a rebellious spirit we are to "take it to the *Church*" to bring the full force of the Church's love on the fallen. While the purpose of Christ's church has many facets it is a sure thing that His church is to be *a place of warfare and discipline*. Within the church we are to be so involved in relationship with one another that we use the gifts that God has given to each of us for the edification and the protection of the body of believers. Within the church we are to hold each other accountable to lives that are worthy of the gospel of Jesus Christ. We need to strengthen and encourage one another toward submissive obedience to His Lordship. For as long as we live we will be in the battle that began before Creation. It is important for us to remember that we have the armor to successfully combat the enemy while here on earth. Most important of all is the fact that this battle against Satan and his lies has already been won!

It is so important for you to know this truth. It is essential that you learn to live in this understanding in faith. That last statement is vital. We desperately need to learn to live in the understanding that the battle has been won! Here's why: If the battle has been ultimately won, we should then run with confidence even in the midst of our struggles here on earth. Walking in faith of the victory won is our part of the sanctification process.

To the Colossians, (Colossians 1:28), the Apostle Paul said that his ministry purpose was to present every man mature in Christ Jesus. This is also our Christian responsibility. Earlier in this same letter to the Colossians Paul prays and shares this encouragement: "For this reason also, since the day we heard of it, we have not ceased to pray for you and to ask that you may be filled with the knowledge of His will in all spiritual wisdom and understanding, so that you may walk in a manner worthy of the Lord, to please Him in all respects, bearing fruit in every good work and increasing in the knowledge of God; strengthened with all power, according to His glorious might, for the attaining of all steadfastness and patience; joyously giving thanks to the Father, who has qualified us to share in the inheritance of the saints in light," (Colossians 1:9-12). This too, is our example as to how we are to approach one another in truth and love.

As Christians we should be constantly striving to become mature in our Dance with the Trinity. We should also be constantly striving to encourage others to come to that same place with us. It is true that we all are infinitely secure and safe, important, and esteemed as children of God. We are all unconditionally loved by a personal God that has set the example of sacrifice through the blood offering of His Son. We have all been filled with a power that has freed us from the snares of temptation by the indwelling of His Holy Spirit.

In our maturity we will become more able to begin to think lofty thoughts of the Most High God. Our maturity should lead us to the point that we ask questions like: "Who is this God?" "How is it that He loves me so perfectly?" "How do I respond to such a love as this?" "Are my thoughts of this God consistent with His word, or do I have an idea of God that isn't true?" As we become more familiar with His word we begin to recognize His attributes and understand His revelation. At the core of His ferocious love is the fact that His Eternal Word, by way of the incarnation, became flesh and dwelt among us. His Spirit lives within us as our guide and our comfort. The Father passionately desires to have us close in intimate relationship.

God does exist in three persons: The Father, The Son, and The Holy Spirit. In these three persons He has given us a slight glimpse of His character. But, we must know that the answers will not come to us easily concerning His nature, His character, and His attributes. We must dig. We must dig deeply seeking God out via prayer, meditation, and study of His Holy Word. We must become as disciplined with the pursuit of God as the discipline associated with a world-class athlete. Our spiritual labor must be a pursuit of God that is purposeful, consistent, and disciplined. One might ask, why is it so important that we labor in the pursuit of God? Mainly the need to labor comes from our human limitations. Let me explain. In early chapters I divided the Trinity (Father, Son, and Holy Spirit) and spoke as though the work of the Three Persons of the Godhead were each different. In chapter three The Holy Spirit's task was that of regeneration. Chapter four discussed The Father as the "Author of Creation." In the fifth chapter the Son's role was clearly redemption. While all of this is true, it can only be true in part. That is, God cannot divide Himself in such a way that one Person of the Godhead works while another Person of the Godhead is inactive. The Scriptures clearly show that the three Persons of the Trinity always act in perfect unity and harmony in all that they do. As humans we are limited in our thoughts to that of humans.

Our attempts to explain God by assigning Him human qualities, not because it is exactly Who He is or what He does, is our best effort in faith to describe the gloriously indescribable. It is true that God has chosen to reveal aspects of His character to us. It is also true that not all people can or will see the brilliance of His glorious nature. Only those who are spiritually prepared to receive His revelation will enter into the Dance. Only those individuals who recognize their spiritual poverty, who mourn over their condition, who approach His throne in meekness, who long for Him with a hunger and thirsting in their souls for righteousness can come to a Holy God. "Blessed are the pure in heart, for they shall see God." Those people will see their divinely jealous God that has invited them to Dance with the Trinity.

In the passage commonly referred to as "The Great Commission," Christ our Savior calls us to maturity in our faith that reaches out to bring others to an intimate relationship with Him. In responding correctly to His command we introduce others to what it means to be at peace with God. *"And Jesus came up and spoke to them, saying, 'All authority has been given to Me in heaven and on earth. Go therefore and make disciples of all the nations, baptizing them in the name of the Father and the Son and the Holy Spirit, teaching them to observe all that I commanded you; and lo, I am with you always, even to the end of the age,'"* (Matthew 28:18-20). I truly hope that you will spend some time thinking deeply about what our Savior has called us to in this passage. In the simplest of terms we are to learn about Him. As we grow and mature in our knowledge, we are to then put our knowledge into practice. In other words, we are to practice living in the wisdom of our Savior. Lastly, but certainly equally important, we are to "go" and make disciples. It is our Christian obligation to share the Good News of Christ's love in both precept and practice as we live out our daily lives.

Gracefully Mature

If we learn to Dance with the Trinity we will have become closer to what it means to be mature in Christ Jesus. This will happen because we will be in Jesus and Jesus will be in us. We will be becoming "one" with Him just as He and the Father are one. Just as the Son is in the Father and the Father is in the Son, our spiritual maturity will cause Christ to be in us and we will be in Him. This maturity then will dictate direction. This spiritual maturity will cause change. It will produce and show fruit as we dance in His presence. As we mature our goal will be the same as that of the Apostle Paul's. Like his ministry, the purpose of our ministry will become modeling Christ as we Dance with the Trinity. In our dance we grow to the point that our deepest desire is to present every man mature in Christ. In other words, we want to help people be complete or completed in Christ Jesus. The goal of learning to Dance with the Trinity, the goal of living out the Gospel is to be in Christ and bring others to that wonderful place.

Through a passionate pursuit of the study of His word we are to become submissively obedient to His teaching. Thus, through the power of the Holy Spirit we develop the "art of living well." As we live this "art," our life becomes an example of what it means to be in the Dance. Consequently we are to teach others and lead them to the Dance. We are to encourage others to find peace with God. We are to be living sacrifices in our effort to move others to the dance floor and show them how to Dance with the Trinity. As we begin to live in Christ we will become unrecognizable to those that used to know us before the transformation of our old nature to the new. The submissively obedient nature we now have in Jesus will confound those that knew us before our transformation and sanctification process had begun.

Because of our position in Christ and our place in His purpose, our lives have meaning. It is also true that our lives matter, that we are valuable, that we are truly significant in our world and in the Kingdom of God. The deepest source of our personal value and significance is that God unconditionally loves us. God continuously pours out His "perfect" love that is unwavering. As the forgiven we have all been placed in God's family and are thus heirs to all that He is.

Living securely in Christ Jesus will have significant impact on all the aspects that have been mentioned related to being created in the image of God. Learning to dance will affect the parts of us that are personal, emotional, volitional, and relational.

The result of being in Christ Jesus and Dancing with the Trinity will be that we will no longer live in a fear of failure in our personal relationships. This truth will exist because we have learned how to live in the commitment to "behave well," to stand firm and to remain objective, compassionate, and even non-defensive in the face of personal attack. This will happen because the threat is now gone. *Nothing can shake the worth a person has in Christ Jesus when they learn to dance.*

Being in Christ Jesus allows us to acknowledge and fully experience the full range of emotions that exist within us in ways that glorify God. It is not that we somehow become exempt to the fullness of emotion in our lives. Even while dancing we can experience intense and excruciating emotional pain, fierce anger, fear that, at the moment, seems overwhelming. We can experience all the intense emotions associated with what it means to be human. However, in Christ Jesus, during the Dance we are always free to do what is right. In the face of these intense emotional experiences we can through our volition choose to be gracefully submissive and mature in our Dance with the Trinity.

While dancing I have the authority and the ability to choose to set my will to follow Christ Jesus. I can now choose to do whatever should be done in any situation because through the indwelling Holy Spirit I have been given strength by Christ to face anything with behavior that is righteous and worshipful.

As a child of God, a person that lives in Christ, and one that is filled with the Holy Spirit we now have a new source of wisdom. In I Corinthians 1:30 it clearly states that Christ has become our wisdom. Paul tells us, in Colossians 2:3, that in Christ are hidden all the treasures of wisdom and knowledge. Did you hear that? Do you understand the message that Paul is giving us about this Christ? Paul in his letters is saying that Christ is absolutely and totally sufficient for us. The message here is that Christ is exclusively appropriate for filling our cup, and when that is all we have in our cup, we are completely and fully His as God has intended. So we enter the Dance!

Our Lives as a Fragrant Offering

"What's that smell?" she asked. "It seems to be coming from the other side of the room where those people are standing."

"Yes, you're right," he said. "Do you know who those people are?" he asked.

"I've seen them before, perhaps a couple of times," she said. "I know that when they are near I feel strength, something positive, and free. What's the smell though? I've never smelled anything like that before. Can you tell what it is?" she asked.

He responded, "It's pleasant and seems to be coming from everywhere at once. It is coming from those people that you suspected as the source. They know Jesus and have learned to live their lives according to His teaching."

She started to softly cry and stated, "If that is what it truly means to follow Christ then please teach me how. It's the sweetest, softest, most perfect fragrance I have ever experienced."

That would be the conversation of those around you if you were Dancing with the Trinity. Your life would be a fragrant offering. The spiritual and emotional climate would change, for the good, just because you entered the room. The soft, sweet fragrance in your life would be the result of you becoming a *"living sacrifice, holy and pleasing to God,"* (Romans 12:1, 2).

Let a person set their heart solely on doing the will of God, and they are instantly free... If we understand that our first and only duty is loving God supremely and loving everyone, even our enemies, then we can enjoy spiritual tranquility (peace with God) under every circumstance. When we live in spiritual tranquility and peace with God we are free to dance, to **Dance with the Trinity.**

Important Notes:

- Either Christians don't know or have forgotten the words of Jesus found in John 17:11, 21 – 23. (Please read that passage.)

- Now that you have read this passage how should this influence the way you interact with other Christ-followers? How does this passage influence the way you interact with God?

- Jeremiah 29:13 says, "And you will seek Me and find Me, when you search for Me with all your heart."

- Now I want to ask you a question that I asked at the end of the first chapter: If Jesus were to pray for you on your behalf, what "one" thing would you most like Jesus to ask the Father to do for you? Jesus has prayed for you and on your behalf. What did He pray? (John 17:11, 21-23)

There are no more Bible studies associated with this book. It's time for you to go and do! Get on the dance floor. Remember Benjamin Franklin said, "Well done is better than well said."

Go! Go Now! Get on the dance floor and dance - *Dance with the Trinity*. Amen

The LAMB
and His Ferocious Love

Part Two

W*hat's In a Name* was the title of a book I purchased some thirty years ago. The entire book is dedicated to names and their meaning. When my children were born this book was read and studied trying to come up with just the right name for each child.

What is in a name? Throughout the Bible the emphasis that is placed on a name, or the naming of a person, is significant. If you were to research the word "name" *(let me suggest* Strong's Exhaustive Concordance of the Bible*)* you would quickly see how often the Bible mentions something about a name, and more specifically the name or names of God. Make no mistake, the emphasis that is placed on the name of Jesus is absolutely astounding.

And Jesus was His name...

Whether there is an ability to cite chapter and verse or not, most followers of Christ can tell you that the Bible states: "that at the name of Jesus every knee should bow, of those who are in heaven, and on earth, and under the earth, and that every tongue should confess that Jesus Christ is Lord, to the glory of God the Father," (Philippians 2:10-11). Those verses are powerful but are truly just a start toward understanding the power and significance that is placed on the name of Jesus throughout the Scriptures.

This Part Two of Chapter 5 is a bit different but no less important. - an alphabetical listing of the *"names"* used to refer to Christ Jesus, nothing more and as you will see nothing less. As you read, note that the names are found throughout the Scriptures in both the Old and the New Testament.

Like anything we do, studying the Bible will get better with practice. Also like anything we practice, some practice days will just be more fun than others. For example, some might not see the value of studying the various genealogies in the Bible. However, you have to recognize that, "All Scripture is inspired by God and profitable for teaching, for reproof, for correction, for training in righteousness; that the man of God may be adequate, equipped for every good work," (2 Timothy 3:16-17). Hebrews 4:12 states: "For the word of God is living and active and sharper than any two-edged sword, and piercing as far as the division of soul and spirit, of both joints and marrow, and able to judge the thoughts and intentions of the heart." It is obvious that every part of the Scriptures has purpose and meaning for us concerning God's revelation.

I would suggest that you read this entire Appendix in one sitting. It shouldn't take that long, but I believe the potential impact of such an exercise will be powerful. When you have time, go back and look up the various scripture references and see how these names of Jesus are used. I believe you will enjoy the exercise, and you will also be amazed at how focused all of Scripture is on the Lamb, the Son of God. Throughout all of Scripture it is the person of Christ Jesus that is the topic. It is

the person of Christ Jesus that is the theme. He is the supreme
subject of each and every book of the New Testament, and He
[Christ] fulfills all the promises of God in the Old Testament.

The Names and Titles Found in the Scriptures for Jesus Christ

All references in this chapter are from the King James Bible

Between each division, I wrote a few poetic lines.

There are twenty-one (21) Names or Titles that begin with

'A'

The Advocate with the Father (I John 2:1)

Aijeleth Shahar (Psalm 22:Title)

An Alien unto My Mother's Children (Psalm 69:8)

Alive for Evermore (Revelation 1:18)

The All, and in All (Colossians 3:11)

The Almighty Which Is (Revelation 1:8)

The Alpha and Omega (Revelation 1:8)

An Altar (Hebrews 13:10)

The Altogether Lovely (Song of Solomon 5:16)

The Amen (Revelation 3:14)

The Angel of the Covenant (Malachi 3:1)

The Angel of God (Genesis 21:17)

The Angel of His Presence (Isaiah 63:9)

The Angel of the Lord (Genesis 16:7)

The Anointed of God (I Samuel 2:35; Psalm 2:2)

Another King (Acts 17:7)

The Apostle of Our Profession (Hebrews 3:1)

The Ark of the Covenant (Joshua 3:3)

The Arm of the Lord (Isaiah 53:1)

The Author of Eternal Salvation (Hebrews 5:9)

The Author of Our Faith (Hebrews 12:2)

Oh, <u>Anointed of God</u>, the One who does heal;
*Search my heart, draw me close, make Your life in me real.**

There are thirty-two (32) Names or Titles that begin with

'B'

The Babe of Bethlehem (Luke 2:12, 16)

The Balm in Gilead (Jeremiah 8:22)

A Banner to Them that Fear Thee (Psalm 60:4)

The Bearer of Glory (Zechariah 6:13)

The Bearer of Sin (Hebrews 9:28)

The Beauties of Holiness (Psalm 110:3)

Before All Things (Colossians 1:17)

The Beginning (Colossians 1:18)

The Beginning of the Creation of God (Revelation 3:14)

The Beginning and the Ending (Revelation 1:8)

The Beloved (Ephesians 1:6)

My Beloved Son (Matthew 3:17)

The Better (Hebrews 7:7)

The Bishop of Your Souls (I Peter 2:25)

The Blessed and Only Potentate (I Timothy 6:15)

The Blessed for Evermore (II Corinthians 11:31)

The Blessed Hope (Titus 2:13)

The Branch (Zechariah 3:8; 6:12)

The Branch of the Lord (Isaiah 4:2)

The Branch of Righteousness (Jeremiah 33:15)

The Branch Out of His Roots (Isaiah 11:1)

The Bread of God (John 6:33)

The Bread of Life (John 6:35)

The Breaker (Micah 2:13)

The Bridegroom of the Bride (John 3:29)

The Bright and Morning Star (Revelation 22:16)

The Brightness of His Glory (Hebrews 1:3)

The Brightness of Thy Rising (Isaiah 60:3)

Our Brother (Matthew 12:50)

A Buckler (Psalm 18:30)

The Builder of the Temple (Zechariah 6:12-13)

A Bundle of Myrrh (Song of Solomon 1:13)

> *Bread of Life, fill my heart, my mind, and my soul*
> *With You as my source I am bound to be whole!*

There are forty (40) Names or Titles that begin with

'C'

The Captain of the Hosts of the Lord (Joshua 5:14-15)

The Captain of Their Salvation (Hebrews 2:10)

The Carpenter (Mark 6:3)

The Carpenter's Son (Matthew 13:55)

A Certain Nobleman (Luke 19:12)

A Certain Samaritan (Luke 10:33)

The Chief Cornerstone (Ephesians 2:20; I Peter 2:6)

The Chief Shepherd (I Peter 5:4)

The Chiefest Among Ten Thousand
(Song of Solomon 5:10)

A Child Born (Isaiah 9:6)

Child of the Holy Ghost (Matthew 1:18)

The Child Jesus (Luke 2:27, 43)

The Chosen of God (I Peter 2:4)

Chosen out of the People (Psalm 89:19)

Christ (Matthew 1:16)

The Christ (I John 5: 1)

Christ Come in the Flesh (I John 4:2)

Christ Crucified (I Corinthians 1:23)

The Christ of God (Luke 9:20)

Christ Jesus (Acts 19:4)

Christ Jesus the Lord (II Corinthians 4:5)

Christ a King (Luke 23:2)

Christ the Lord (Luke 2: 11)

Christ Our Passover (I Corinthians 5:7)

Christ Risen from the Dead (I Corinthians 15:20)

The Chosen of God (Luke 23:35)

A Cleft of the Rock (Exodus 33:22)

A Cluster of Camphire (Song of Solomon 1:14)

The Comforter (John 14:16-18)

A Commander to the Peoples (Isaiah 55:4)

Conceived of the Holy Spirit (Matthew 1:20)

The Consolation of Israel (Luke 2:25)

The Corn of Wheat (John 12:24)

Counselor (Isaiah 9:6)

The Covenant of the People (Isaiah 42:6; 49:8)

The Covert from the Tempest (Isaiah 32:2)

The Covert of Thy Wings (Psalm 61:4)

The Creator (Romans 1:25)

The Creator of the Ends of the Earth (Isaiah 40:28)

A Crown of Glory (Isaiah 28:5)

The Chosen of God, The Crucified – yet lives,
Since the dawn of Creation Your love always gives.

<u>There are seventeen (17) Names or Titles that begin with</u>

'D'

My Darling (Psalm 22:20)

David (Matthew 1:17)

The Day (II Peter 1:19)

The Daysman Betwixt Us (Job 9:33)

The Dayspring from on High (Luke 1:78)

The Daystar to Arise (II Peter 1:19)

His Dear Son (Colossians 1:13)

That Deceiver (Matthew 27:63)

My Defense (Psalm 94:22)

The Deliverance of Zion (Joel 2:32)

My Deliverer (Psalm 40:17)

The Desire of All Nations (Haggai 2:7)

Despised by the People (Psalm 22:6)

The Dew of Israel (Hosea 14:5)

A Diadem of Beauty (Isaiah 28:5)

The Door of the Sheep (John 10:7)

Dwelling Place (Psalm 90:1)

A shield and a sword, You are <u>My Defense</u>,
From a selfish human mind this love makes no sense.

There are seventeen (17) Names or Titles that begin with 'E'

Mine Elect (Isaiah 42:1)

Eliakim (Isaiah 22:20)

Elijah (Matthew 16:14)

Emmanuel (Matthew 1:23)

The End of the Law (Romans 10:4)

The Ensign of the People (Isaiah 11:10)

Equal with God (Philippians 2:6)

The Eternal God (Deuteronomy 33:27)

That Eternal Life (I John 1:2)

The Everlasting Father (Isaiah 9:6)

An Everlasting Light (Isaiah 60:19, 20)

An Everlasting Name (Isaiah 63:12)

Thy Exceedingly Great Reward (Genesis 15:1)

His Excellency (Job 13:11)

The Excellency of Our God (Isaiah 35:2)

Excellent (Psalm 8:1, 9)

The Express Image of His Person (Hebrews 1:3)

Equal with God You are of the Trinity,
You are Holy, You are lovely, part of Divinity.

There are thirty-eight (38) Names or Titles that begin with

'F'

The Face of the Lord (Luke 1:76)

The Fairer than the Children of Men (Psalm 45:2)

Faithful (I Thessalonians 5:24)

Faithful and True (Revelation 19:11)

The Faithful and True Witness (Revelation 3:14)

A Faithful Creator (I Peter 4:19)

A Faithful High Priest (Hebrews 2:17)

A Faithful Priest (I Samuel 2:35)

The Faithful Witness (Revelation 1:5)

A Faithful Witness Between Us (Jeremiah 42:5)

A Faithful Witness in Heaven (Psalm 89:37)

My Father (Psalm 89:26)

A Father of the Fatherless (Psalm 68:5)

The Feast (I Corinthians 5:8)

My Fellow (Zechariah 13:7)

The Finisher of the Faith (Hebrews 12:2)

The First and the Last (Revelation 1:8)

The First Begotten (Hebrews 1:6)

The Firstborn (Hebrews 12:23)

The Firstborn among Many Brethren (Romans 8:29)

The Firstborn of the Dead (Revelation 1:5-
    KJV "begotten")

The Firstborn of Every Creature (Colossians 1:15)

Her Firstborn Son (Luke 2:7)

The First Fruit (Romans 11:16)

The First-Fruits of Them that Sleep
   (I Corinthians 15:20)

Flesh (John 1:14)

The Foolishness of God (I Corinthians 1:25)

Foreordained before the Foundation of the World
   (I Peter 1:20)

The Forerunner (Hebrews 6:20)

Fortress (Psalm 18:2).

The Foundation Which Is Laid (I Corinthians 3:11)

The Fountain of Life (Psalm 36:9)

The Fountain of Living Waters (Jeremiah 17:13)

The Free Gift (Romans 5:15)

The Friend of Publicans and Sinners (Matthew 11:9;
   Luke 7:34)

A Friend that Sticketh Closer than a Brother
   (Proverbs 18:24)

The Fruit of the Earth (Isaiah 4:2)

The Fruit of Thy Womb (Luke 1:42)

Fullers' Soap (Malachi 3:2)

*The First and the Last, The Beginning and the End;
   You are past, present, future — You always have been.*

There are forty-seven (47) Names or Titles that begin with

'G'

The Gift of God (John 4:10)

A Gin (Isaiah 8:14)

A Glorious High Throne from the Beginning
(Jeremiah 17:12)

A Glorious Name (Isaiah 63:14)

Glory (Haggai 2:7)

My Glory (Psalm 3:3)

The Glory as of the Only Begotten of the Father
(John 1:14)

The Glory of God (Romans 3:23)

The Glory of His Father (Matthew 16:27; Mark 8:38)

God (Revelation 21:7)

God Who Avengeth Me (Psalm 18:47)

God Blessed Forever (Romans 9:5)

God Who Forgavest Them (Psalm 99:8)

Our God Forever and Ever (Psalm 48:14)

The God of Glory (Psalm 29:3)

The God of Israel (Psalm 59:5)

The God of Jacob (Psalm 46:7)

The God of My Life (Psalm 42:8)

The God of My Mercy (Psalm 59:10)

God in the Midst of Her (Psalm 46:5)

God Manifest in the Flesh (I Timothy 3:16)

God of My Righteousness (Psalm 4:1)

God of My Salvation (Psalm 18:46; 24:5)

God of My Strength (Psalm 43:2)

God with Us (Matthew 1:23)

A Good Man (John 7:12)

The Goodman of the House (Matthew 20:11)

Good Master (Matthew 19:16)

The Good Shepherd (John 10:11)

The Governor Among Nations (Psalm 22:28)

Great (Jeremiah 32:18)

The Great God (Titus 2:13)

A Great High Priest (Hebrews 4:14)

A Great Light (Isaiah 9:2)

A Great Prophet (Luke 7:16)

That Great Shepherd of the Sheep (Hebrews 13:20)

Greater (I John 4:4)

A Greater and More Perfect Tabernacle (Hebrews 9:11)

Greater Than Our Father Abraham (John 8:53, 57-58)

Greater Than Our Father Jacob (John 4:12)

Greater Than Jonah (Matthew 12:41)

Greater Than Solomon (Matthew 12:42)

Greater Than the Temple (Matthew 12:6)

Guest (Luke 19:7)

Our Guide Even Unto Death (Psalm 48:14)

The Guide of My Youth (Jeremiah 3:4)

The Guiltless (Matthew 12:7)

Greater – *YES!!!*

There are forty-one (41) Names or Titles that begin with

'H'

The Habitation of Justice (Jeremiah 50:7)

Harmless (Hebrews 7:26)

An He Goat (Proverbs 30:31)

The Head of All Principality and Power
(Colossians 2:10)

The Head of Every Man (I Corinthians 11:3)

The Head of the Body, the Church (Colossians 1:18)

The Head of the Corner (I Peter 2:7)

The Health of My Countenance (Psalm 42:11)

The Heir (Mark 12:7)

Heir of All Things (Hebrews 1:2)

My Helper (Hebrews 13:6; Psalm 32:7)

The Helper of the Fatherless (Psalm 10:14)

A Hen (Matthew 23:37)

The Hidden Manna (Revelation 2:17)

My Hiding Place (Psalm 32:7)

A Hiding Place from the Wind (Isaiah 32:2)

The High and Lofty One Who Inhabiteth Eternity
(Isaiah 57:15)

An High Priest (Hebrews 5:5)

An High Priest after the Order of Melchisedec
(Hebrews 5:10)

An High Priest Forever (Hebrews 6:20)

My High Tower (Psalm 18:2)

The Highest Himself (Psalm 87:5)

An Highway (Isaiah 35:8)

Holy (Isaiah 57:15)

Thy Holy Child Jesus (Acts 4:27)

Thine Holy One (Acts 2:27)

The Holy One and Just (Acts 3:14)

The Holy One of Israel (Psalm 89:18)

That Holy Thing Which Shall Be Born of Thee
(Luke 1:35)

Holy to the Lord (Luke 2:23)

Our Hope (I Timothy 1:1)

The Hope of Glory (Colossians 1:27)

The Hope of His People (Joel 3:16)

The Hope of Israel (Acts 28:20)

The Hope of Their Fathers (Jeremiah 50:7)

The Horn of David (Psalm 132:17)

The Horn of the House of Israel (Ezekiel 29:21)

A Horn of Salvation (Luke 1:69)

A House of Defense (Psalm 31:2)

A Householder (Matthew 20:1)

Her Husband (Revelation 21:2)

'My Helper' You are, 'My Helper' are You;
Draw me close, change my heart, make me ever true.

There are five (5) Names or Titles that begin with
'I'

I Am (John 18:6)

The Image of the Invisible God (Colossians 1:15)

Immanuel (Isaiah 7:14)

Innocent Blood (Matthew 27:4)

Isaac (Hebrews 11:17, 18)

'Immanuel' God with us,
It's only on You that I place my trust.

There are seventeen (17) Names or Titles that begin with
'J'

The Jasper Stone (Revelation 4:3)

Jeremiah (Matthew 16:14)

Jesus (Matthew 1:21)

Jesus Christ (Hebrews 13:8)

Jesus Christ the Lord (Romans 7:25)

Jesus Christ, the Son of God (John 20:31)

Jesus of Galilee (Matthew 26:69)

Jesus of Nazareth (John 1:45)

Jesus of Nazareth, the King of the Jews (John 19:19)

A Jew (John 4:9)

John the Baptist (Matthew 16:14)

Joseph's Son (Luke 4:22)

The Judge of All the Earth (Genesis 18:25)

The Judge of the Quick and the Dead (Acts 10:42)

A Judge of the Widows (Psalm 68:5)

The Just One (Acts 7:52)

This Just Person (Matthew 27:24)

With all Your names so precious, so wonderful, so Holy,
With all Your titles so important, so dominant, so awesome,
I see You smile and say – just call me <u>Jesus</u>.

There are twenty-two (22) Names or Titles that begin with

'K'

Thy Keeper (Psalm 121:5)

The Kindness and Love of God (Titus 3:4)

Another King (Acts 17:7)

The King Eternal (I Timothy 1:17)

The King Immortal (I Timothy 1:17)

The King in His Beauty (Isaiah 33:17)

The King Forever and Ever (Psalm 10:16)

The King Invisible (I Timothy 1:17)

The King of All the Earth (Psalm 47:7)

The King of Glory (Psalm 24:7,8)

The King of Heaven (Daniel 4:37)

The King of Israel (John 1:49)

King of Kings (Revelation 19:16)

The King of Peace (Hebrews 7:2)

The King of Righteousness (Hebrews 7:2)

King of Saints (Revelation 15:3)

The King of Salem (Hebrews 7:2)

The King of Terrors (Job 18:14)

King of the Jews (Matthew 2:2)

The King Who Cometh in the Name of the Lord
   (Luke 19:38)

The King's Son (Psalm 72:1)

The Kinsman (Ruth 4:14)

Thy Keeper, keeper of my soul,
I bless Your name for making me whole.

There are fifty-eight (58) Names or Titles that begin with

'L'

A Ladder (Genesis 28:12)

The Lamb (Revelation 17:14)

The Lamb of God (John 1:29)

The Lamb Slain from the Foundation of the World
     (Revelation 13:8)

The Lamb That Was Slain (Revelation 5:12)

The Lamb Who Is in the Midst of the Throne
     (Revelation 7:17)

The Last (Isaiah 44:6)

The Last Adam (I Corinthians 15:45)

The Lawgiver (James 4:12)

A Leader (Isaiah 55:4)

The Life (John 14:6)

The Lifter-Up of Mine Head (Psalm 3:3)

The Light (John 1:7)

The Light of Men (John 1:4)

The Light of the City (Revelation 21:23)

The Light of the Glorious Gospel of Christ
     (II Corinthians 4:4)

The Light of the Knowledge of the Glory of God
     (II Corinthians 4:6)

The Light of the Morning (II Samuel 23:4)

The Light of the World (John 8:12)

The Light of Truth (Psalm 43:3)

A Light to Lighten Gentiles (Luke 2:32)

A Light to the Gentiles (Isaiah 49:6)

The Lily among Thorns (Song of Solomon 2:2)

The Lily of the Valleys (Song of Solomon 2:1)

The Lion of the Tribe of Judah (Revelation 5:5)

The Living Bread (John 6:51)

The Living God (Psalm 42:2)

Lord - despotes (II Peter 2: 1)

Lord - kurios (John 13:13)

Lord - rabboni (Mark 10:51)

Lord Also of the Sabbath (Mark 2:28)

My Lord and My God (John 20:28)

The Lord and Saviour (II Peter 1:11)

Lord Both of the Dead and Living (Romans 14:9)

The Lord from Heaven (I Corinthians 15:47)

Lord God Almighty (Revelation 16:7)

The Lord God of the Holy Prophets (Revelation 22:6)

Lord God of Israel (Psalm 41:13)

Lord God of Truth (Psalm 31:5)

Lord God Omnipotent (Revelation 19:6)

The Lord God Who Judgeth Her (Revelation 18:8)

The Lord, Holy and True (Revelation 6:10)

Lord Jesus (Romans 10:9)

Lord Jesus Christ (James 2:1)

The Lord Mighty in Battle (Psalm 24:8)

The Lord of All the Earth (Joshua 3:11)

The Lord of Glory (I Corinthians 2:8)

The Lord of the Harvest (Matthew 9:38)

The Lord of Hosts (Psalm 24:10)

O LORD Our Lord (Psalm 8:1,9)

Lord of Lords (I Timothy 6:15)

Lord of Peace (II Thessalonians 3:16)

The Lord of the Vineyard (Matthew 20:8)

The Lord of the Whole Earth (Psalm 97:5)

The Lord's Christ (Revelation 11:15)

The Lord's Doing (Matthew 21:42)

The Lord Strong and Mighty (Psalm 24:8)

Lowly in Heart (Matthew 11:29)

__The Lamb__ of sacrifice shedding blood on a cross;
Innocence died by His plan for all that were lost.

There are forty-two (42) Names or Titles that begin with

'M'

Magnified (Psalm 40:16)

Our Maker (Psalm 95:6)

A Malefactor (John 18:30)

The Man (John 19:5)

A Man Approved of God (Acts 2:22)

A Man Child (Revelation 12:5)

The Man Christ Jesus (I Timothy 2:5)

A Man Gluttonous (Matthew 11:19)

The Man Whose Name Is the Branch (Zechariah 6:12)

The Man of Sorrows (Isaiah 53:3)

The Man Whom He Hath Ordained (Acts 17:31)

Manna (Exodus 16:15)

Marvelous in Our Eyes (Matthew 21:42)

The Master - didaskalos (John 1.1:28)

Master - epistates (Luke 5:5)

Your Master - kathegetes (Matthew 23:10)

The Master of the House - oikodespotes (Luke 13:25)

Master - rabbi (John 4:31)

The Meat Offering (Leviticus 2:1)

The Mediator (I Timothy 2:5)

The Mediator of a Better Covenant (Hebrews 8:6)

The Mediator of the New Covenant (Hebrews 12:24)

The Mediator of the New Testament (Hebrews 9:15)

Meek (Matthew 11:29)

Melchizedek (Genesis 14:18)

A Merciful and Faithful High Priest (Hebrews 2:17)

His Mercy and His Truth (Psalm 57:3)

Mercyseat (Hebrews 9:5; I John 2:2)

The Messenger of the Covenant (Malachi 3:1)

Messiah (Daniel 9:26)

Messiah the Prince (Daniel 9:25)

Mighty (Psalm 89:19)

The Mighty God (Isaiah 9:6)

The Mighty One of Jacob (Isaiah 49:26; 60:16)

The Minister of Sin (Galatians 2:17)

A Minister of the Circumcision (Romans 15:8)

The Minister of the Heavenly Sanctuary (Hebrews 8:1-3)

A More Excellent Name (Hebrews 1:4)

The Morning Star (Revelation 2:28)

The Most High (Psalm 9:2; 21:7)

The Mouth of God (Matthew 4:4)

The Mystery of God (Colossians 2:2)

You are beautiful, You are lovely, so sublime that You are;
You are holy, You are precious, You are
The Morning Star.

There are five (5) Names or Titles that begin with

'N'

A Nail Fastened in a Sure Place (Isaiah 22:23)

A Name above Every Name (Philippians 2:9)

A Nazarene (Matthew 2:23)

Thy New Name (Revelation 3:12)

A Nourisher of Thine Old Age (Ruth 4:15)

A Nail Fastened in a Sure Place so secure and steadfast;
You are The Rock, A Cornerstone, the First and the Last.

There are nine (9) Names or Titles that begin with

'O'

An Offering and a Sacrifice to God (Ephesians 5:2)

The Offspring of David (Revelation 22:16)

Ointment Poured Forth (Song of Solomon 1:3)

The Omega (Revelation 22:13)

His Only Begotten Son (John 3:16)

The Only Begotten of the Father (John 1:14)

Only Potentate (I Timothy 6:15)

The Only Wise God (I Timothy 1:17)

An Owl of the Desert (Psalm 102:6)

An Owl of the Desert, what a strange way to describe;
The God, become Man with Whom I abide.

There are forty (40) Names or Titles that begin with

'P'

Our Passover (I Corinthians 5:7)

The Path of Life (Psalm 16:11)

A Pavilion (Psalm 31:20)

Our Peace (Ephesians 2:14)

The Peace-Offering (Leviticus 3:1)

A Pelican of the Wilderness (Psalm 102:6)

A Perfect Man (James 3:2)

The Person of Christ (II Corinthians 2:10)

Physician (Luke 4:23)

The Pillar of Fire (Exodus 13:21, 22)

The Place of Our Sanctuary (Jeremiah 17:12)

A Place of Refuge (Isaiah 4:6)

A Plant of Renown (Ezekiel 34:29)

A Polished Staff (Isaiah 49:2)

Poor (II Corinthians 8:9)

My Portion (Psalm 119:57)

The Portion of Jacob (Jeremiah 51:19)

The Portion of Mine Inheritance (Psalm 16:5)

The Potter (Jeremiah 18:6)

The Power of God (I Corinthians 1:24)

Precious (I Peter 2:7)

A Precious Cornerstone (Isaiah 28:16)

The Preeminence (Colossians 1:18)

A Price (I Corinthians 6:20)

The Price of His Redemption (Leviticus 25:52)

A Priest Forever (Psalm 110:4)

The Priest of the Most High God (Hebrews 7: 1)

A Prince and Saviour (Acts 5:3 1)

The Prince of Life (Acts 3:15)

The Prince of Peace (Isaiah 9:6)

Prince of Princes (Daniel 8:25)

The Prince of the Kings of the Earth (Revelation 1:5)

The Prophet (John 7:40)

A Prophet Mighty in Deed and Word (Luke 24:19)

The Prophet of Nazareth (Matthew 21:11)

A Prophet without Honor (Matthew 13:57)

One of the Prophets (Matthew 16:14)

The Propitiation for Our Sins (I John 2:2)

Pure (I John 3:3)

A Purifier of Silver (Malachi 3:3)

When my body feels bad, a Physician I call,
You are the great healer, You reign over all.

There are two (2) Names or Titles that begin with

'Q'

Of Quick Understanding (Isaiah 11:3)

A Quickening Spirit (I Corinthians 15:45)

Of Quick Understanding, the One that knows all;
From The Beginning to End on Whose name I call.

<u>There are fifty-three (53) Names or Titles that begin with</u>

'R'

Rabbi (John 3:2)

Rabboni (John 20:16)

Rain upon the Mown Grass (Psalm 72:6)

A Ransom for All (I Timothy 2:6)

A Ransom for Many (Matthew 20:28)

The Red Heifer without Spot (Numbers 19:2)

My Redeemer (Job 19:25)

Redemption (I Corinthians 1:30; Luke 21:28)

The Redemption of Their Soul (Psalm 49:8)

A Refiner's Fire (Malachi 3:2)

Our Refuge (Psalm 46:1)

A Refuge in Times of Trouble (Psalm 9:9)

A Refuge for the Oppressed (Psalm 9:9)

A Refuge from the Storm (Isaiah 25:4)

Our Report (Isaiah 53:1)

A Reproach of Men (Psalm 22:6)

Their Resting Place (Jeremiah 50:6)

A Restorer of Thy Life (Ruth 4:15)

The Resurrection and the Life (John 11:25)

The Revelation of Jesus Christ (Revelation 1:1)

Reverend (Psalm 111:9)

A Reward for the Righteous (Psalm 58:11)

Rich (Romans 10:12)

The Riches of His Glory (Romans 9:23)

The Riddle (Judges 14:14)

Right (Deuteronomy 32:4)

The Righteous (I John 2: 1)

A Righteous Branch (Jeremiah 23:5)

The Righteous God (Psalm 7:9)

The Righteous Lord (Psalm 11:7)

My Righteous Servant (Isaiah 53:11)

The Righteous Judge (II Timothy 4:8)

A Righteous Man (Luke 23:47)

Righteousness (I Corinthians 1:30)

The Righteousness of God (Romans 10:3)

A River of Water in a Dry Place (Isaiah 32:2)

The Rock (Matthew 16:18)

The Rock that Is Higher Than I (Psalm 61:2)

The Rock of Israel (II Samuel 23:3)

A Rock of Offense (Romans 9:33)

The Rock of My Refuge (Psalm 94:22)

The Rock of His Salvation (Deuteronomy 32:15)

The Rock of Our Salvation (Psalm 95:1)

The Rock of Thy Strength (Isaiah 17:10)

The Rod (Micah 6:9)

A Rod out of the Stem of Jesse (Isaiah 11:1)

The Root of David (Revelation 5:5)

A Root of Jesse (Romans 15:12; Isaiah 11:10)

A Root out of Dry Ground (Isaiah 53:2)

The Root and Offspring of David (Revelation 22:16)

The Rose of Sharon (Song of Solomon 2:1)

A Ruler (Micah 5:2)

Why do I write the things that I do?
You're My Redeemer, my worship and my praises are for You.

There are ninety-four (94) Names or Titles that begin with
'S'

The Sacrifice for Sins (Hebrews 10:12)

A Sacrifice to God (Ephesians 5:2)

My Salvation (Psalm 27:1)

The Salvation of God (Luke 2:30; 3:6)

The Salvation of Israel (Jeremiah 3:23)

A Samaritan (John 8:48)

The Same Yesterday, Today and Forever (Hebrews 13:8)

A Sanctuary (Isaiah 8:14)

A Sardius Stone (Revelation 4:3)

The Saving Strength of His Anointed (Psalm 28:8)

Saviour (Titus 2:13)

The Saviour of All Men (I Timothy 4:10)

The Saviour of the Body (Ephesians 5:23)

The Saviour of the World (John 4:42; I John 4:14)

The Scapegoat (Leviticus 16:8; John 11:49-52)

The Scepter of Israel (Numbers 24:17)

The Scepter of Thy Kingdom (Psalm 45:6)

The Second Man (I Corinthians 15:45)

Secret (Judges 13:18)

The Secret of Thy Presence (Psalm 31:20)

The Seed of Abraham (Galatians 3:16)

The Seed of David (Romans 1:3; II Timothy 2:8)

The Seed of the Woman (Genesis 3:15)

The Sent One (John 9:4)

Separate from His Brethren (Genesis 49:26)

Separate from Sinners (Hebrews 7:26)

The Serpent in the Wilderness (John 3:14)

My Servant (Isaiah 42:1)

A Servant of Rulers (Isaiah 49:7)

My Servant the Branch (Zechariah 3:8)

A Shadow from the Heat (Isaiah 25:4)

The Shadow of the Almighty (Psalm 91:1)

The Shadow of a Great Rock (Isaiah 32:2)

A Shelter (Psalm 61:3)

My Shepherd (Psalm 23: 1; Isaiah 40:11)

Shepherd of Israel (Psalm 80:1)

Our Shield (Psalm 84:9)

Shiloh (Genesis 49:10)

Shoshannim (Psalm 45:69)

A Sign of the Lord (Isaiah 7:11)

Siloam (John 9:7)

Sin (II Corinthians 5:21)

A Snare to the Inhabitants of Jerusalem (Isaiah 8:14)

The Son (Matthew 11:27)

His Son from Heaven (I Thessalonians 1:10)

A Son Given (Isaiah 9:6)

The Son of Abraham (Matthew 1:1)

The Son of David (Matthew 1:1)

The Son of God (John 1:49)

The Son of Joseph (John 1:45)

The Son of Man (John 1:51)

The Son of Mary (Mark 6:3)

The Son of the Blessed (Mark 14:61)

The Son of the Father (II John 3)

The Son of the Freewoman (Galatians 4:30)

The Son of the Highest (Luke 1:32)

The Son of the Living God (Matthew 16:16)

The Son of the Most High (Mark 5:7)

A Son over His Own House (Hebrews 3:6)

The Son Who Is Consecrated for Evermore
  (Hebrews 7:28)

My Song (Isaiah, 12:2)

A Sower (Matthew 13:4, 37)

A Sparrow Alone upon the Housetop (Psalm 102:7)

That Spiritual Rock (I Corinthians 10:4)

A Star out of Jacob (Numbers 24:17)

My Stay (Psalm 18:18)

A Stone Cut out of the Mountain (Daniel 2:45)

A Stone Cut without Hands (Daniel 2:34)

The Stone of Israel (Genesis 49:24)

A Stone of Stumbling (I Peter 2:8)

The Stone Which the Builders Refused (Psalm 118:22)

The Stone Which the Builders Rejected (Matthew 21:42)

The Stone Which Was Set at Nought (Acts 4:11)

A Stranger (Matthew 25:35)

My Strength (Isaiah 12:2)

The Strength of Israel (I Samuel 15:29)

The Strength of My Life (Psalm 27:1)

A Strength to the Needy in Distress (Isaiah 25:4)

A Strength to the Poor (Isaiah 25:4)

Strong (Psalm 24:8)

A Strong Consolation (Hebrews 6:18)

A Stronghold in the Day of Trouble (Nahum 1:7)

A Strong Lord (Psalm 89:8)

My Strong Refuge (Psalm 71:7)

My Strong Rock (Psalm 31:2)

A Strong Tower (Proverbs 18:10)

A Strong Tower from the Enemy (Psalm 61:3)

A Stronger than He (Luke 11:22)

A Stumbling Block (I Corinthians 1:23)

The Sun of Righteousness (Malachi 4:2)

A Sure Foundation (Isaiah 28:16)

The Sure Mercies of David (Isaiah 55:3; Acts 13:34)

A Surety of A Better Testament (Hebrews 7:22)

A Sweet-Smelling Savor (Ephesians 5:2)

You're all that I have, You're My Strength and My Stay;
You're The Lord of Creation, what more can I say?

There are nineteen (19) Names or Titles that begin with

‘T’

A Tabernacle for a Shadow (Isaiah 4:6)

The Tabernacle of God (Revelation 21:3)

Teacher (Matthew 10:25)

A Teacher Come from God (John 3:2)

The Temple (John 2:19)

The Tender Grass (II Samuel 23:4)

A Tender Plant (Isaiah 53:2)

The Tender Mercy of God (Luke 1:78)

The Testator (Hebrews 9:16,17)

The Testimony of God (I Corinthians 2:1)

This Treasure (II Corinthians 4:7)

The Trespass Offering (Leviticus 5:6)

A Tried Stone (Isaiah 28:16)

The True Bread from Heaven (John 6:32)

The True God (Jeremiah 10:10)

The True Light (John 1:9)

The True Vine (John 15:1)

The True Witness (Proverbs 14:25)

The Truth (John 14:6)

"I am the Way, the Truth and Life...," (John 14:6).

There are seven (7) Names or Titles that begin with the letter
‘U’

Undefiled (Hebrews 7:26)

Understanding (Proverbs 3:19)

The Unknown God (Acts 17:23)

The Unspeakable Gift (II Corinthians 9:15)

The Urim and Thummin (Exodus 28:30)

The Upholder of All Things (Hebrews 1:3)

Upright (Psalm 92:15)

Sometimes I'm discouraged, feel rejected and uptight.
You are always courageous, secure, and <u>Upright</u>.

There are seven (7) Names or Titles that begin with
'V'

The Veil (Hebrews 10:20)

The Very God of Peace (I Thessalonians 5:23)

Very Great (Psalm 104:1)

A Very Present Help in Trouble (Psalm 46:1)

The Victory (I Corinthians 15:54)

The Vine (John 15:5)

The Voice (Revelation 1:12)

Without You we're lost, our-lives have no shine,
We are the branches, and You are <u>The Vine.</u>

There are twenty-four (24) Names or Titles that begin with
'W'

A Wall of Fire (Zechariah 2:5)

The Wave-Offering (Leviticus 7:30)

The Way (John 14:6)

The Way of Holiness (Isaiah 35:8)

The Weakness of God (I Corinthians 1:25)

A Wedding Garment (Matthew 22:12)

The Well of Living Waters (John 4:14)

The Well of Salvation (Isaiah 12:3)

Wisdom (I Corinthians 1:25)

The Wisdom of God (I Corinthians 1:24)

A Wise Master Builder (I Corinthians 3:10)

Witness (Judges 11:10)

My Witness (Job 16:19)

The Witness of God (I John 5:9)

A Witness to the People (Isaiah 55:4)

Wonderful (Judges 13:18)

Wonderful Counselor (Isaiah 9:6)

The Word (John 1:1)

The Word of God (Revelation 19:13)

The Word of Life (I John 1:1)

A Worm and No Man (Psalm 22:6)

Worthy (Revelation 4:11; 5:12)

That Worthy Name (James 2:7)

Worthy to be Praised (Psalm 18:3)

> *Worthy to be Praised* it is You and You alone;
> You are the One worthy to sit on The Throne.

There are two (2) Names or Titles that begin with

'X'

X as Chi, The Traditional Symbol of Christ

X as an Unknown Quantity (Revelation 19:12)

Red and yellow, black and white, You are precious in our sight;
Some say You are brown, others say white; perhaps You are olive,
or black like the night.

Regardless of color or race You are King, You are the X
(the Christ) over everything.

There are two (2) Names or Titles that begin with

'Y'

The Yokefellow (Matthew 11:29-30)

The Young Child (Matthew 2:11)

You came as a babe and lived The Young Child,
Offer peace to us all, You are tender and mild.

There are four (4) Names or Titles that begin with

'Z'

Zaphnath-paaneah (Genesis 41:45)

The Zeal of the Lord of Hosts (Isaiah 37:32)

The Zeal of Thine House (John 2:17; Psalm 69:9)

Zerubbabel (Zechariah 4:7,9)

Your energy is endless, raising You from the grave;
You are The Zeal of Thine House, Your praises be raised.

The Total Names and Titles for Jesus the Christ is 675

The Other Side

Baptisms, Maple Trees, and Birthdays

W e caught up with the author the other day outside a small sidewalk bistro in downtown Winter Park, Florida, and asked if we could conduct a brief interview to learn a bit about his background and life. It was an interesting discussion and quite different from the usual biographical data obtained from similar interviews that we have conducted.

Interviewer: "Dr. Bell, I wonder if you have a few minutes to answer a couple of questions?"

Rye: "Sure, I would love that. But, please call me Rye. What are your questions?"

Interviewer: "We are interested in asking you a few questions to find out a little bit about your background and your life. Would that be okay with you?"

Rye: "Absolutely, but you need to know that I find it so difficult to respond to personal questions such as: 'What do you do?' 'Where do you live?' 'What do you do in your spare time?' etc... I never know exactly what to say. I hope you will ask me important questions like: 'What makes me smile?' 'What stimulates me intellectually, and what stirs my soul?' Questions like: 'What can I do now that I couldn't do as a child?' I'm sorry. It's your interview. Go ahead and ask your questions. However, you need to know that I get nervous with things like this and usually just ramble. I promise to try and stay focused and perhaps this time things will turn out differently!"

Interviewer: "Well, honestly we did have some of those biographical-type questions that we wished to ask of you. But, we could ask some of your questions as well! In fact, why don't I start with one of your questions?"

Interviewer: "So, what does make you smile?"

Rye: "What makes me smile? Many things. I love to watch children playing pretend. Their innocence and imagination are such a wonder to me. I smile when I speak to a member of the geriatric population. They carry so much life experience, and I can see the wisdom in their eyes. I smile at animal names like yellow-bellied sapsucker, google-eyed bass, pig-nosed turtle, duck-billed platypus, hog-nosed snake, and many, many others (God really has a sense of humor). My eyes brighten (I believe you can smile with your eyes) when I take in Creation. Part of my personal dance is enjoying all that God has made, and I am in no hurry to pass it by."

Interviewer: "Where do you live?"

Rye: "Merely existing is not what I would define as living. True living can take place anywhere and tends to be controlled by one's attitude. For me part of dancing with God comes from understanding that I am only visiting this planet and have indeed been designed for a much grander place. I work hard to remind myself to enjoy the moment and thus *live* in the moment. I tend to treat myself well. I truly enjoy rich conversation, meaningful books, watching baptisms, singing praises to God, and, yes even a fine cigar and a glass of top-shelf brandy on rare occasions. Genuine living requires discipline and concentration. But, I have discovered that as I practice the "art of living well," the wonderful gift of life that God has provided is one that is filled with excitement, emotion, challenge, and adventure. Living is an act of relationship with my Creator, and thus I am drawn to The Dance and find life (thus live) in the midst of this beautiful relationship."

Interviewer: "Ok (*I think?*). Let me get back to one of your suggested questions. So what stimulates you intellectually? What stirs your soul?"

Rye: "I am intellectually stimulated by classical music, good books, and long conversation that is sweet and purposeful. My soul is stirred when I realize that God has just allowed me to live this day by faith and I have tasted just a hint of His power and goodness. The excitement in my soul cannot be contained when I witness a baptism. It is such a beautiful moment."

Interviewer: "What can you do now that you couldn't do as a child?"

Rye: "When I was a child I lived in a home that had a large pantry in the kitchen. For reasons that baffled my young mind the cookies were placed on the very top shelf of that pantry. There wasn't a dining room chair or even the step stool from the laundry room that could make me tall enough to reach those delicious temptations. Well, I can now reach the top shelf of the pantry, and more importantly, I can eat as many cookies as I want. I'm the boss, and no one can tell me when or how many cookies I can eat! Alas, if I show little or no discipline I will be subject to finding new clothes in larger sizes than before. Also, there's that whole health thing that one needs to be conscious of. So while I am now capable of such a thing, this new ability "to do" might not be beneficial. Isn't that the way it always is?

When anyone behaves irresponsibly and in disobedience they find that they are bound to a life of sin, bondage, and death. But, for those who choose to conduct themselves responsibly and in obedience to God, they dance. As one dances they find life and live in His freedom."

Interviewer: "I liked that last answer. Let me flip it around and ask: What could you do as a child that you can't do now?"

Rye: "When I was little there was a Maple tree in my backyard. It was definitely a tree that God had planted for a small boy just like me. The limbs were perfect for climbing, and I could really go high! Some of my fondest memories are of those times in the top of that old Maple tree. On a cool, breezy fall night just before the sun would set you could usually find me in that tree. I was up there enjoying the moment. I was usually singing to myself (I like to sing). The song was brand new because I was making it up as I sang. They were all beautiful songs that brought me much joy and a smile to my heart. I still love to sing, and if I were to be absolutely honest I would admit to still loving to climb trees and really going high! Now the problem is that if I climb to the top of the tree and sing the song that makes my heart smile someone will see the old, bald man up there and get concerned. They might even call on the authorities for help. (Bummer)."

Interviewer: "What do you do?"

Rye: "This strikes me as an interesting question. It doesn't address whether one does something well, rarely rises above average, or just limps along as a miserable failure. It appears to only be interested in activity. There is a huge part of me that is thankful that the person asking these questions does not concern themselves with my success and/or failures. With that thought in mind I will share that I begin each day asking myself what appears to be a simple question on the surface, but usually creates tremendous challenges for me as I keep my focus. The question is this: Am I going to cooperate with God today in such a way that will ensure that my life will work, or am I going to passionately pursue God today whether my life works or not? To ask myself this question and to make honest attempts to land on the second option requires that I learn to live by faith. It is in this style of living that I am able to truly know God, experience His love, and gracefully dance. When I exercise the first option I have found that I tend to miss God entirely and rob myself of enjoying His Holy presence in my life. Even though I realize this I find that I **DO** option number one much more than I care to admit. By God's grace I am learning how to **DO** the second option more often. This makes me hungry for my time to come of glorification, being perfected in His presence. Maranatha *(Come soon Lord Jesus)!*"

Interviewer: "Where do you serve?"

Rye: "The Christian scriptures call us to "...have the attitude of Christ," (Phil. 2:5). Serving should not be a place but an attitude that is revealed in action. I personally enjoy serving those closest to me in my life. It brings me tremendous joy to minister to a need that a loved one of mine has and watch them receive this gift of my love. In many ways this becomes a selfish act on my part because I receive a joy in this activity that escapes me in many other facets of life. I wish my actions were altruistic but alas even when serving my flesh is sometimes the victor. Maybe they'll never discover my selfishness and just think I'm being a good guy."

Interviewer: "Why are you here?"

Rye: "Of all the questions that have been asked this is both the simplest and at the very same time the most complex. I am here to glorify God with my life. My life should be a living sacrifice unto Him. My actions should rise up as sweet incense to His nostrils. While I have no problem proclaiming these things and at times getting parts of this directive accomplished, I often fail. I am still a man in need of a Savior."

Interviewer: "This has been a truly different style of interview. But, I have to admit I have enjoyed our conversation. Is there anything else that you think we would find interesting about you?"

Rye: "I am just an old Tennessee 'hillbilly' at heart. I love my University of Tennessee Volunteers and follow them with a high degree of interest in all of their sporting activities. It is important that I explain my deep affection for the University of Tennessee. Sam Darden is a person that I admire. I consider him both a mentor and personal friend. Sam recently retired after 38 years of faithful service as the campus Minister for the Christian Student Fellowship on the campus of the University of Tennessee. It was Sam that encouraged me to pursue advanced education in the field of counseling. It was also Sam that challenged me to think in terms of the Biblical revelation in regard to coming alongside hurting individuals and families. It was at the CSF that I began learning how to fall in love with Jesus. While my "Dance" was awkward initially, for the first time in my life I stepped onto the dance floor with the sole intent of learning how to let my God lead me through the art of living well. So you see it was on the campus of The University of Tennessee that I found Jesus!

I love music. God has placed music in my soul, and many times my dance, my praise is through music. Urban Gospel music stirs my soul, and I sing in an Urban Gospel Group. However, I listen to a variety of genres and play a couple of stringed instruments.

My Father was in my life for 10 ½ years before he died from a massive heart attack. He was a good man, and the loss was significant. While the time we spent together was short, the quality of that time was as good as the best and better than the rest! This man poured his life into mine. In our short time together he taught me what it means to be a man of God and modeled it daily. He was my teacher. I was his "Sunshine." We were the best of friends. I love and miss him dearly.

I am the proud husband of Becky. She is God's perfect and holy gift to me. She is the one that brings stability to my life and excites my soul. She makes me smile. Becky is the perfect example of "that one true love" I spoke about in chapter two of this book. Proverbs 18:22 says, "He who finds a wife finds a good thing, and obtains favor from the Lord." She has the gift from God of being a *good* wife. I have the joy of being the recipient of her gift. Becky is my favor from the Lord. I am not sure how she does it, but she pours her life into mine in such a way as to successfully fill-in all the gaps that I have (and I have so many). She is God's perfect, chosen tool to complete me. Led by the Holy Spirit she uses her life to encourage, support, love, strengthen, and serve as a healing salve to my soul. With Becky I am always protected. She is my friend.

I have five children, two biological (a son and a daughter) and three adopted (two sons and a daughter). It has been a blessing and a joy to be Daddy to all five. My two oldest children are married and are creating their own families. I now have a son-in-law, a daughter-in-law, and two grandchildren (maybe more on the way!).

It is my opinion that birthdays should be special and celebrated with vigor! At this point I have had 58 of them. It seems that it should be important for a person to do things on their birthday that they don't usually get to do on the other 364 un-birthdays during the year. I try to do things on my birthday like fly an ultra-light, go snorkeling, parasail, jump off cliffs into mountain streams, or jump off draw bridges over the inter-coastal waterways. You might find me hanging out at a James Taylor or Jack Johnson concert. Or, "get'in down wif my old bad sef," at a Temptations and Four Tops live performance. I might even rent a huge "super-slide" and set it up in my backyard. Then I would play and fellowship all afternoon with 50 of my closest adult friends (that was really fun!). I love to eat my fill of bakery-made birthday cake. I eat from a big red plate that says: "You Are Special Today" (I have a matching coffee mug as well). I think the celebration to mark the event of your birth should always be extra special!

Wow, that wasn't so bad. Aren't you glad I stayed to the point and didn't ramble?"

Rye

About the Author

Rye Bell has been working in the field of Biblical Guidance for more than 30 years serving on the staff of both small and large congregations. He has taught advanced counseling courses at the college level and has successfully managed the program and fiscal operations of several private ministry organizations and departments of major health care corporations.

While working closely with church congregations, his specialty is Biblically based support for the congregations and their staff. This support is offered through one-on-one contacts with individuals and families, training interested believers to become mentors within the congregation, and setting up the design and operations of "one-another-type" ministries to lead in the Biblical idea of shepherding the flock of believers. He also works within the Christian community through Church Leadership training, seminars, and spiritual retreats.

Dr. Bell has served as the President and/or Administrative Director of four in-patient psychiatric hospitals, as well as VP of medical/surgical hospitals. Under his leadership one of his facilities was named top 100 hospitals in the country with the psychiatric service line also being given that top honor.

As an ordained Pastor, Rye received his Doctor of Philosophy (Religion and Society) from Oxford Graduate School; Masters of Science (Social Work) from the University of Tennessee; and a Bachelor of Science (Education) from the

University of Tennessee. He is also a member of the Oxford Society of Scholars and was a Charter member of the American Association of Christian Counselors.

Dr. Bell lives in Florida with his wife Becky and three of his five children. The two oldest children are married with growing families of their own. He counsels daily with individuals and families, and also travels conducting Biblically based conferences and workshops on a variety of topics.

Post Script

As a gifted counselor and conference speaker, Dr. Bell has spoken throughout the United States and many foreign countries. Conference topics include:

Walk with God Weekend

(A weekend conference dedicated to realizing God's Holy presence in your life and your obedient response)

...If you are beset by an especially obstinate sin, you may be on the verge (even this weekend) of seeing God's grace displayed in your life. Although you may now be preoccupied with your struggle, you may soon become preoccupied with your God.

Purifying Your Marriage

(A weekend experience dedicated to enriching your marriage)

...What would have to happen for you to come to the point in your individual life and within the corporate life of your marriage to truly believe that protecting your marriage relationship is right? It is right purely because of God's goodness. The focus is how to put your marriage under God's Holy authority by learning to: remain loyal; communicate well; fight fair; pray together; forgive from the heart; and become one in the Spirit.

People of Encouragement

(A one day seminar on becoming shepherds of God's flock)

...This seminar is designed mainly for Church Leadership (both professional and lay positions). The focus is learning how to provide Biblical care and discipleship for members of your congregation at various levels, i.e., front line listeners providing care for one's soul; Biblical Guidance from the authority of the Scriptures; and recognizing when to refer to the Spiritually solid, trained professional.

Dance with the Trinity

(A half day seminar on developing relationship with God and Man)

...This seminar is designed to teach what the Scriptures have to say about relationship with Man and with God. The main focus is on how we were created in the image of God for His good pleasure and as a result are to be in holy relationship with the body and with Him. Learning about the *One Another Principle* and *Biblical Forgiveness* are key points that will help to live life abundantly!

~

**For information on booking one of these seminars
or to schedule Dr. Bell to speak at a church
or community gathering contact**

www.dancewiththetrinity.com.

Dance with the Trinity

ISBN 978-1-935434-06-1

Dr. Rye Bell